The Life Story of Ann Lowe: America's First Black Woman Haute Couture Designer



Library of Congress Control Number: TXU-2-288-048

ISBN: 9798828551668



Any references to historical events, real people, or places are used fictitiously. Names, characters, and places are products of the author's imagination.

Front cover and Book Design by Belton Media©

First printing edition 2022 in the United States

Belton Media

www.beltonmedia.co

*Written, Published, and Created*
*by*

BELTON MEDIA
Educating While Entertaning

# ANN LOWE

***America's First Black Woman Haute Couture Designer and Fashion's Best-Kept Secret***

Written By

**PIER ANGELA BELTON**

*Ann Lowe's life story lies beneath layers of fabric woven together through adversity, triumphs, and personal tragedy. But Ann's story is just one thread of countless unsung Black Americans whose contributions to America have either faded or never made it into American History.*

*Ms. Lowe's life serves as a reminder that when we ignore parts of our history, we ignore parts of ourselves. So, to embrace who we are, we must first learn where we have been, where we are now, and what we must do to get to where we are going.*

*Today, we honor America's first black haute couture designer, Ann Lowe, by telling her fascinating life story and admiring her extraordinary designs. May her name and contributions to the fashion industry finally take their rightful place in American history.*

*Thank you, Lord, for guiding and seeing me through this journey. I could not have done this without your help. You are worthy to receive glory and honor forever.*

*This book is dedicated to all the gifted black American women past and present who designed, sewed, labored, and created extraordinary designs throughout American history but never received the recognition or compensation they deserved. We honor their talent, determination, and accomplishments.*

# Col·ored Cou·ture

**/ˈkələrd/ /ko͞oˈto͝o(ə)r/**

---

**Definition:**

*A phrase used to describe a negro woman seamstress or dressmaker who designed clothing for high society white women from the 1900s until the 1960s. Her designs were well-known, but her name usually wasn't.*

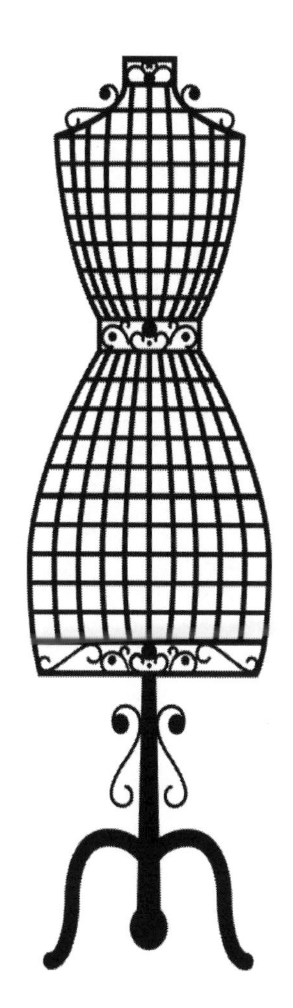

Special Thanks to:

*Linda D.*

*(Ann Lowe's great-granddaughter)*

*Thank you for everything!*

---

In Fond Memory

of

Margaret Powell

Writer/Historian

---

*In Loving Memory*

*of*

*Sadie "Mama Sadie" Tatum*

*1929 – 2021*

*A Beautiful Colored Couture Queen*

*To My Aunt Lovonya M. Dejean*
*Thank You For Teaching And*
*Showing Me How To Love Our*
*History.*

For centuries, the splendor of black history has been interwoven continuously from the shores of Africa right to the shores of America. After arriving in America, Black people may have been stripped of their clothing but definitely not their style. The thread that has sewn their heritage together and held it tight for centuries does not tear easily.

Black people are cut from the same cloth as their ancestors, complete with beauty, talent, strength, and dignity. They are created in a wide range of colors, each shade exquisite on its own, made in the perfect image of the One who created them.

The love that binds them together in unity is their gift to the world, and when it is evident, people can't help but be drawn to their magnetic energy. The interfacing layer of their humanity and community will continue to give strength and structure to the next generation and thousands of other generations to come.

Although Black people have been treated unjustly and, on many occasions, have been cast aside, they always find the strength and courage to rise. And no matter how many times they had to restitch or patch up their wounds from injustice, they still adhered to the same pattern of excellence and with the same exquisite aura that characterizes them. While their fabric has been damaged and shredded too many times to count, their beauty still shines bright like the sun.

The hem of the garment has always been their hook and eye, for it gives them the power and fortitude to overcome any circumstances. And while the clothing on their backs may change, who they are clothed to be, wonderfully and fearfully made, will remain the same forever. This is the essence of black excellence.

# Table of Contents

# INTRODUCTION

Many unsung black American women have played a vital role in shaping the fashion industry in America. Unfortunately, their stories have either gone unnoticed or been forgotten by American history. Ann Lowe, the granddaughter of former slaves, is one of those women whose story has not received the recognition it deserves.

The name Ann Lowe isn't immediately recognizable in the world of fashion, but it certainly should be. Once described as "Society's best-kept secret" by the Saturday Evening Post in 1964, in recent years, Ann's designs have reemerged, causing a whole new generation to admire her work. *F*rom her early days of dressing Southern belles in *Montgomery, Alabama,* to her prime years of dressing East Coast elites in New York, Ann's sewing gift allowed her to break down color barriers in the fashion industry. Her talent gave her a longevity career in a predominately white industry, where opportunities for blacks were scarce and black female designers were all but nonexistent. But against all the odds, she persevered and became a sought-after designer for the rich and famous.

Ann worked during a period in American history when social and political conditions created an oppressive environment for African

Americans. When Jim Crow laws (a racial system that relegated African Americans to the status of second-class citizens) stood as an obstacle for Ann, she didn't let it stop her. She used her skills to become a successful fashion designer with limited resources, inadequate education, and no formal business experience.

During her 50-year career, Ann had her label and was the first African American haute couture designer to open a store on the prestigious Fifth Ave in New York. Ann's fairytale-like gowns were popular from the 1920s to the 1960s and usually sold for one thousand dollars apiece. Her gowns were popular because she offered her customers dresses that enhanced their beauty rather than eclipsed it. She sold her designs in high-end stores like Henri Bendel, Saks Fifth Ave, Neiman Marcus, and I. Magnin. She became the first African American head designer at Saks Fifth Ave (Adam Room). Her style and creativity impressed French fashion designer Christian Dior and legendary Hollywood costume designer Edith Head.

Ann's designs made the pages of *Vogue, Town & Country,* and other popular fashion magazines. Movies stars and jazz singers wore her designs. Women who wore her gowns said they loved wearing them because they made them feel beautiful. Ann was the go-to designer for America's socially prominent and wealthy families at the height of her career, including the du Ponts, the Roosevelts, the

Rockefellers, the Vanderbilts, and the Kennedys. Yet, the fashion industry rarely acknowledged Ann's talent.

One of Ms. Ann's most notable accomplishments was designing the wedding dress for the future first lady, Jackie Bouvier Kennedy. Creating Jackie Bouvier's wedding dress should have been a career-defining moment for Ann. Still, the future first lady was said to have credited "a colored woman" with creating the famous gown, neglecting to identify Ann by name. This would not be the first time or last time Ann was overlooked or not credited for her designs. So, unfortunately, the designer behind the iconic Kennedy creation remained somewhat an unsung hero.

Today, Ann Lowe is no longer "society's best-kept secret" or "fashion's best-kept secret." She is finally receiving the recognition she deserves by having her iconic designs on display at the National Museum of African American History and Culture, the Smithsonian, the Metropolitan Museum of Art, and The Museum at FIT. Each collection seems truly fitting to pay tribute to a once-unknown designer.

Ann Lowe's life story lies beneath layers of fabric woven together through adversity, triumphs, and personal tragedy. But her story is just one thread of countless unsung African Americans whose contributions to America have either faded or never made it into

American History. To ignore parts of our history is to ignore parts of ourselves. So, to embrace who we are, we must first learn where we have been, where we are now, and what we must do to get to where we are going.

# Chapter One

# WHERE IT ALL STARTED

***"It may be our hands that are laboring, but God is the One at work."– Plantation Slave***

To understand the significance of the role of the black seamstress in America, we must first look at her past. When slaves arrived in America, they were stripped of what little traditional clothing they had and given clothing made from osnaburg fabric (heavy linen material made from flax and hemp). Slaves cared little for this material. They found it to be constricting and very uncomfortable. Slaves were not supplied with a lot of clothing. They were provided with one item that was decent enough to wear. If slaves were hired out, they usually received more clothing: two suits, one pair of shoes, and one blanket.

However, this was not a general rule; it could vary from plantation to plantation. On many plantations, boys wore short pants until they were ten years old, then transitioned to wearing long pants. Girls

later wore adult dresses when they started menstruating. Plain leather shoes and sometimes hats were also included in allotments.

The most common practice was distributing clothes in a twice-a-year allotment, with domestic or house slaves receiving higher-quality clothing than field slaves, who wore the plainest and coarsest dress. By the nineteenth century, with the rise of cotton production, blends such as jean cloth became more common and allowed owners to provide slaves with untailored and ready-made clothing.

The material of the clothing was coarse and far from being comfortable. Shoes that were given to slaves usually lasted only a few weeks. Slaves were required to keep their clothes clean. Slaves usually washed their clothing in a nearby stream after working in the cotton fields. Afterward, they would build a fire and dry them. Sometimes, slaves wore their clothes until they were worn out, without ever washing them.

When slave clothing became torn or worn out, they were given to a slave woman, who was taught how to use a needle and thread by an older slave seamstress living in the master's house. It was the slave's job to be creative and somehow work miracles in repairing old, worn-out clothing.

This would be the first introduction of the black seamstress, who played a very significant role during slavery. Not limited to only sewing, the black seamstress had to have various skills to maintain

her position in her master's house. She had to know how to sew, but she was also expected to know how to spin, weave, wash, and iron clothes.

While the black seamstress's skills with a needle and thread kept her busy in the master's house, her hard work was rarely acknowledged, compensated, or appreciated. She was smart, and she knew how to use her skills to survive her hostile environment.

During this time, women slaves were subordinate not only because of their race but also their gender. They usually worked in two distinct areas: fieldwork, where they performed primarily unskilled agricultural tasks, or domestic work, within the household structure. The skilled slave seamstress would be a member of the latter division of labor.

On a few Southern plantations, where the master was generous, some slave seamstresses benefited from cash payments, from which they someday yearned to purchase their freedom. But even if a slave could buy their freedom, they were still subject to brutal abuse by white folks who would ignore that they were free. During this time, human rights for slaves were non-existent.

And the working conditions, whether in the house or the fields, were brutal and cruel. The slave seamstress constantly knew that she could lose her position in the master's house any day and work in the fields with no warning.

Therefore, she paid close attention to every detail of her job, often going beyond her daily duties to secure her position in the big house. Everything the slave seamstress knew about sewing, she made sure she passed down to the next generation, hoping to make a better life for themselves.

When the door of slavery closed, the door of entrepreneurship opened up for former slaves. The former slave seamstress relied on her sewing skills to support her family. Making less than a dollar a day, she struggled to survive in a racially divided America.

Even decades after slavery ended, the transition from slave woman to free woman was difficult for the slave seamstress. Her journey was often filled with racism, financial setbacks, injustice, and lack of opportunities. And that was the journey of America's first black woman haute couture designer, Ann Lowe.

# Chapter Two

# A DESIGNER IS BORN

***"My mother said I came out of her womb ready to sew."***

***– Ann Lowe***

On December 14, 1898, Ann Lowe was born in Clayton, Alabama. She was the great-granddaughter of a skilled seamstress slave and a white plantation owner. Her mixed-race grandmother, Georgia Tompkins, made clothes for her plantation mistress before she was given clemency from slavery after being purchased by a freedman and carpenter named General Cole. Georgia and General married in 1860. A year later, they had a daughter named Jane. Jane grew up watching her mother sew, and by the time she was 11 years old, she was exceptionally skilled with embroidery. To help her family earn money, Jane would assist her mother with dressmaking for Clayton's prominent society women.

At sixteen, Jane married Ann's father, Jack Lowe. Jack, Jane, Georgia, and General moved to Montgomery, Alabama, looking for a better life. Within a year, Jane and Georgia had established themselves as society dressmakers in Montgomery, Alabama. Their

clientele included political wives and their daughters. Jack and General worked as construction workers to make ends meet.

"My family was doing quite well for freed black people living in the south during the 1870s. They owned their land, which some white men tried several times to take from them. They grew their own vegetables and plowed their own fields. They were very self-reliant and very proud people. And every Sunday, you would find them attending the only black Baptist church in Montgomery," said Ann's great-granddaughter, Linda Dixon, whom Ann adopted her grandmother, Ruth Williams Alexander.

These were happy times for the Coles and Lowes. Jane and Jack welcomed their first daughter, Sallie, two years into their marriage. A few years later, they welcomed their second daughter, Ann. By the age of five, Ann showed an interest in dressmaking when spending hours creating fabric flower adornments for her hair. Her mother and grandmother realized that the gift of design also ran through her veins. Designing fabric flowers would later become Ann's signature style. She always credited her family for teaching her everything she knew about sewing. "She learned all about sewing from her mother and grandmother," National Museum of American History Curator Emeritus Nancy Davis said. "Ann was really gifted, but she was also part of this exceptional lineage of great seamstresses... and competent ones."

By the late 19th century, after the Reconstruction period, laws were set up to implement segregation. These laws were called the "Jim Crow laws." Jim Crow laws were a collection of state and local statutes that legalized racial segregation. Named after a Black minstrel show character, the laws—which existed for about 100 years, from the post-Civil War era until 1968—marginalized African Americans by denying them the right to vote, hold jobs, and get an education or other opportunities.

Those who attempted to defy Jim Crow laws often faced arrest, fines, jail sentences, violence, and death. As the Cole family prospered, they faced racial resentment from white people in their community. "My great-grandmother talked about seeing Klansmen come to her house and threatening to hurt her father if he didn't give up his land to them. He stood his ground with his shotgun in his hand. They left him alone after discovering that the city's white mayor liked him because he did carpentry work for him practically for pennies. It was a terrifying time for black people," said great-granddaughter Linda.

Segregation was a major part of Ann's young life and most of her adult life. When Ann was six years old, she started attending a segregated school in Montgomery. Ann was taught that she could not go to certain areas for fear of being raped or killed as a young child. She witnessed firsthand the cruelty of a racially divided

environment. Stores in downtown Montgomery featured signs reading “Colored Only” or “White’s Only.” “It wasn’t unusual for my great-grandmother to witness a cross burning on a nearby neighbor’s front lawn or to be told to walk on the opposite side of the street when white people were walking by. She was always cautious of her surroundings, never knowing if she would be spat on or beaten. I don’t think she ever forgot the fear she felt like a little girl walking down those segregated streets of Montgomery,” said great-granddaughter Linda.

Many years later, her cautious behavior would turn into pure pride when she would walk up and down the streets of Fifth Avenue in New York as one of the first black female designers to own a dress shop on the prestigious avenue. She still experienced racism on Fifth Ave, but it was unlike the racism she experienced down south.

When a gifted Ann was thirteen years old, her parents decided it was time for her to leave school and help around the house. It wasn’t unusual for black children to quit school to support their families to make ends meet during this era. “It was hard for her parents to take her out of school because they knew the power of a good education, but at the time, they needed her to help out around the house,” said great-granddaughter Linda. Ann received an education of a lifetime at home by working in the family business of dressmaking, which prepared her for one of the few vocations a black woman could have to support herself.

In 1912, at fourteen, Ann married Lee Cone, a local tailor, twelve years older than her. Her family wasn't thrilled about her marrying Lee, but Ann didn't care. She dreamed of having a marriage like her parents and thought Lee was the right person to make that happen. Due to family pressures, her marriage started a little rocky, but Ann was committed to making her marriage work.

The following year after getting married, Ann and Lee welcomed a son, Arthur Lee. Ann was overjoyed becoming a mother. In an interview with Sepia magazine in 1955, Ann talked about how much her son changed her life. "My life immediately changed for the better after having my son. I never knew I could love someone so much. Everything I've ever done was for him to have a better life," said Ann. To help make ends meet in her household, Ann continued to work as a seamstress with her grandmother, mother, and older sister, Sallie, at their successful dressmaking business in Montgomery, Alabama.

# Chapter Three

# A FAMILY AFFAIR

***"Every woman in my family could sew extremely well. Sewing was in our blood." – Ann Lowe***

The family business was doing well. In 1914, Ann's family was commissioned to make ball gowns for the governor's wife, the First Lady of Alabama, Lizzie Kirkland O'Neal, and her daughters. This commission was an enormous opportunity for the ladies. It was a chance for them to show the socialites of Montgomery how skilled they were with a needle and thread.

Like any other time, when there was a particular order to create elaborate ball gowns, the women would sit together and discuss design ideas. Each woman had a specific role to play in designing dresses. Ann would sketch the dresses and cut out the patterns, Sallie would structure the dresses, Janie would do the embroidery, while Georgia would finish up the gowns with hemming and tending to the small details.

Making these fancy ball gowns required hard work and many long hours, something Ann's husband didn't particularly like. Years later, she spoke about this in an interview with Sepia magazine in 1966, "My first husband, Lee, wanted a stay-at-home wife – and I obeyed him for a while, but when my mother became ill, I had to be there for her," said Ann.

The gowns for the First Lady of Alabama and her daughters were almost complete when Jane suddenly became extremely ill. Jane was confined to her bed while the others worked tirelessly to finish the gowns for the ball. Jane made Ann promise her they would finish those dresses, and Ann promised that they would. They were almost done when Jane's health took a turn for the worst. Jane died surrounded by her family. Her death devastated sixteen-year-old Ann. Jane was not only her mother, but she was also her best friend.

Ann was struggling with grief for her mother. Knowing how much this order meant to her mother, Ann didn't want to let her down, so she dried her eyes and pushed through her pain to finish the job. "It was my first big test in life," Ann recalled in Sepia magazine in 1966, "I remember it was Christmas time, and there were several unfinished gowns in our house. There was a big affair coming up, the Governor's Ball on New Year's Eve, and the ladies were in a terrible panic that their dresses wouldn't be ready on time. My family worked around the clock to finish those dresses on time," said Ann. This order was financially important for Ann and her family,

but it was also crucial for Ann to carry out her mother's dying wishes to finish the gowns and deliver them on time.

Still reeling from grief, Ann and her family successfully finished the four gowns on time and delivered them to Alabama's First Lady, O'Neal. This situation was Ann's first professional triumph. It gave her the feeling "that there was nothing I couldn't do when it came to sewing," Ann once said. The day after the ball, Ann, Sallie, and Grandmother Georgia waited to read what the local newspapers had to say about their dresses. If the high-society women who attended the ball loved their dresses, that meant more business for Ann and her family. They said a prayer and hoped for the best. Their prayer was answered when Alabama's First Lady, O'Neal, mentioned that she and her daughters' "dresses were designed by the Cones/Lowes of Montgomery County." With that much-needed shout-out, their gowns became the talk of the town. Ann, Sallie, and Georgia could not have been happier, but the success came as a bittersweet moment. Ann was delighted, but she wished her mother was there to enjoy their accomplishment. The family business was now in high demand, with orders pouring in from other counties outside Montgomery County.

# Chapter Four

# THE RESPECT YOU GIVE

***"I grew up during intense, horrifying racial violence and deliberate, sustained political oppression of black folks."***

***– Ann Lowe***

While Ann and her family were making a name for themselves in high society circles for white women, they couldn't escape the fact that Black men and women were still being lynched in Alabama. This was a vulnerable time for black communities across the country. Klansmen were burning down black people's houses, torching their businesses, and killing black men and women for no apparent reason. A white person could kill a black person in broad daylight and be home for dinner. Even worst, there were no laws to protect black folks from this kind of cruelty. Black lives had no value. Many can argue that the same sentiment applies to black people in America today.

Ann found it challenging to work within a segregated system during this time while remembering her place in a racially divided Montgomery. While some white people treated her with respect, many did not. Ann had her share of high-class white women who refused to buy from her because she was black. Then some white women even went as far as buying Ann's gowns but didn't give her credit for her designs. They instead recognized less talented white seamstresses working in the same area. Situations like this would become a recurring problem for Ann throughout her career. When Ann found out what was going on, she became furious.

Whereas her mother and grandmother would have settled for this behavior, Ann saw things differently. If Ann felt she was being exploited or disrespected, she refused to serve them. She once overheard two prominent women in town calling her a nigger. When the regular seamstress couldn't sew their dresses for an upcoming ball, they went to Ann to get their dresses made. "My great-grandmother told them this nigger woman is all booked up, but you're welcome to come back another time," laughed great-granddaughter Linda. "My great-grandmother was playing a risky game because it was unheard of for a black woman to refuse service to white women. She could have been jailed or something worse," said great-granddaughter Linda.

Thankfully, the incident did not cause any problems for Ann or her business. It did her some good. The white women who once refused

to buy from her became intrigued by the little black woman who dared to turn them down. Those same ladies who once rejected her finally came around. Many of them became some of Ann's biggest customers. After the incident, Ann realized that if she had compromised her services after hearing them call her a nigger, she would surrender to that name. No matter the consequences, she wasn't willing to do that.

With Ann being the head of the family business, she relied on her grandmother, her sister Sallie, who took care of the money side of the company, and a neighbor to help her out. Like many women who owned their own business and had a family to care for, Ann found balancing her professional life and her personal life both rewarding and exhausting at the same time. Because of this, her marriage to Lee suffered terribly. Lee wanted a stay-at-home wife, and she was not willing to give up what she loved doing the most, and that was sewing. Not able to work things out, she divorced Lee after three years of marriage.

Within months of terminating her marriage, Ann's grandmother, Georgia, died, and her sister, Sallie, got married. Without her family and her neighbor helping her, Ann closed the family business. As a single parent with no husband and no job, Ann struggled with figuring out her next career move. All she knew was sewing, so she got a job as a seamstress at a black-owned cleaner. She thought

that's where she would work forever, but God had other plans for her.

# Chapter Five

# A CHANGE IS COMING

***"I knew God had a plan for my life; I just needed to find it."***

***– Ann Lowe***

A chance meeting in 1915 at a local department store in Montgomery would change Ann's life forever. She describes the encounter that changed her life in Ebony magazine, "Before my divorce, I was feeling enslaved. My great-grandmother was enslaved, her every move controlled by others. My grandmother, for a good part of her life, was enslaved. I decided I was not going to be enslaved. So, let me tell you how God works. I was in the "colored only" section, looking through some old fabric bins, and I felt someone's eyes following me. This was not unusual, for we Negros are always being watched when we're in public, but I knew the owners of this store, and I had never felt threatened there.

"Still, on that day, I knew I was being watched. Slowly, I looked around for some low-life man who might be eyeing me. There was

no one. It was just me, an elderly woman leaning on her cane as she and a sales clerk examined some dismal-looking suits and a smartly-dressed white woman across the store. I went back to my looking. Soon, I felt the eyes on me again. I could hear the sales clerk and the older woman deep in conversation. Still, I had the feeling of being watched. Who was this well-dressed woman, and why was she watching me? I turned as far away from her as possible, settled my countenance into a sweet smile, and abruptly turned to catch her off guard. Instead, she caught me off guard, for she was just four feet from me, with a genuinely sweet smile on her face.

"I must have looked startled, for she quickly apologized and introduced herself. "Hi, my name is Mrs. Josephine Edwards Lee, and I'm from Tampa," she told me. "She said she had never seen a colored girl so well dressed." I thanked her for the compliment, and then she said, "there isn't anyone there who can sew like what you have on." Ann continues, "She was unable to find a quality seamstress who could keep up with the needs of her four active daughters, so she offered me a job as her live-in dressmaker, and of course, I said yes," said Ann. "I believed what was happening was a sign from God. My world changed immediately. I could hardly believe it. Here was a chance to make all the lovely gowns I'd always dreamed of. So, I went home, packed up my baby, got on that Tampa train, and sought my freedom. It was the best decision

I've ever made, and I thank God for giving me the courage to do it," said Ann. (*The Tampa Bay Times Article - 1955.)*

The move to Tampa proved to be good for Ann and Arthur. With Mrs. Lee's high society connections, Ann's career was on the fast track to success. She later recalled that the years she spent in Tampa were the happiest time. She explained in *Ebony*, "Being in Tampa allowed me to grow artistically. The different scenery in Tampa forced me to use different patterns and prints in my designs. Before, I was using soft colors, but with the colorful landscape of Tampa, I began using bright, bold colors," said Ann. Her new designs were a hit with Mrs. Lee and her friends. Women from Tampa's surrounding areas started coming to Ann when they realized she could create sophisticated haute couture—at down-home prices.

Having an "Ann's Designs" dress quickly became a status symbol. An associate curator at the Met Costume Institute, Jessica Regan, explains why she believes Ann's dresses became so famous. "It was her surface embellishments. The miniature carnations with organza petals, each one minutely hand finished. But the interior structure of a dress was just as important to her. Invisible tacking stitches keep the layers of the fabric moving together; a lightly boned bodice holds the bosom stable on a dance floor. Her emphasis on a perfected fit made her clients feel secure."

Ann was feeling entirely secure with her growing clientele. Ann had Mrs. Lee to thank for all her success. "She was my guardian angel. She was kind enough to purchase all of the materials necessary, she provided room and board for me, and she and Arthur paid me a great salary. I didn't want for anything except to be with my dear sister, Sallie," said Ann in an interview with the *Amsterdam Newspaper* in 1957. Sewing for the Lee family and other women in town allowed Ann to save a sizeable chunk of her earnings, which she wanted to use to further her education. "I always knew how important getting a good education was for Negros. Like so many other black folks of my age, I didn't have the opportunity to complete my education because I had to help out my family. I believe the decision to take me out of school at an early age hurt my parents. So, when I had an opportunity to go back to school for dressmaking courses, I did it," said Ann.

## Chapter Six

# SCHOOL DAZE

***"As a Negro woman, it seems like I was always having to prove myself, even when my work did all the talking."– Ann Lowe***

In 1917, Ann left Tampa to attend sewing courses at S.T. Taylor School of Design in Manhattan, New York. Mrs. Lee helped Ann pay for her tuition and a place for her and Arthur to stay in New York. Ann found a reliable babysitter for Arthur while she attended school. Ann was excited about being in New York. She hoped that her skin color wouldn't be an issue in New York as it had been in Alabama and Florida. Unfortunately, she was wrong.

As the only Black student at a segregated school, Ann endured a lot of racism from classmates. She talked about her experience with a journalist from *Ebony* in 1966, "The school's director, who was French, almost didn't take me when he found out I was a Negro. The whole idea to admit a Negro girl to a high-class fashion school was absurd," laughed Ann. "The director didn't believe I had the $1,500 for the course—he just laughed. When I showed him my bankbook,

he stopped laughing, but he still didn't believe that I could learn what he was teaching there," said Ann. It's interesting that Harvard's tuition then was one hundred and fifty dollars, and that S. T. Taylor School of Design was a thousand five hundred dollars. Who knew that sewing classes would cost more than academic courses? Times have changed.

The classes at S.T. Taylor School of Design were challenging for Ann, not because of the work but because of her classmates. In the same article with *Ebony*, she described this period in her life as a "very lonely and difficult time." She often wrote letters to her sister, Sallie, telling her how cold and rude her classmates were. Most of the students refused to work or study with her. "The other girls said that they wouldn't work in the same room with me, so he set me off in a room by myself," said Ann. So, she worked and studied alone in a separate classroom the entire time she was at school. This wasn't the only problem Ann had to deal with. There were more horrendous things going on as well. She was constantly receiving death threats from students. As a safety precaution, the janitor of the school, who was a black man, would walk Ann to her classes. "I was pretty shaken up when I read a note on my desk that said, 'nigger go home.' One student left a mannequin at my desk with a noose tied around its neck with the words "die nigger" written on it. If I used scissors or touched any fabrics, some students would refuse to touch them after me. As if that wasn't enough, I couldn't use the white students'

bathrooms; I had to use the janitor's bathroom in the school's basement. No human being should have been treated like that," said Ann.

Although her experience at school was challenging, she didn't allow the hatred to intimidate her to the point of quitting. Instead, she used that negativity to excel in her classes. Ann's work, which featured meticulous techniques on stitching and embroidery, which she learned from her mother and grandmother, really impressed her teacher. "When my teacher saw my work, he began taking samples to show the other students. Before I knew it, they were coming to my room to watch me," said Ann. As a skilled and fast learner, Ann finished the one-year curriculum in six months, recalling years later that her teacher explained his offer for early completion by telling her, "There is nothing more than I can teach you. You are excellent."

After graduating with honors from S.T. Taylor School of Design, Ann stayed in New York to explore employment opportunities. In 1966, Ann told the *Oakland Tribune* that after she graduated from S.T. Taylor, she worked part-time as an assistant dressmaker in a Manhattan dress shop for several months, sewing together garments from pre-cut pieces. Ann's vision eventually was to open a dress shop in New York, but with few business connections and no long-term opportunities, she and Arthur returned to Mrs. Lee's household in Tampa.

## Chapter Seven

# GOING BACK TO TAMPA

***"I don't believe in wasting anything, especially opportunities."***

***– Ann Lowe***

In 1919, within months of returning to Tampa, Mrs. Lee rented a small workspace in a segregated part of Tampa for Ann to design dresses. Lee and her high-society friends flooded Ann with dress orders. Still using her once married name and her nickname, Annie, she opened a dress shop in Tampa, *Annie's Dresses.* And just like that, Ann was back in business. Once again, her clientele comprised of Tampa's wealthiest women. In a year, Ann's professional life was looking bright, and so was her love life. In 1920, Ann married her second husband, a hotel bellman named Caleb West. Ann's family moved to a lovely African American residential area outside Tampa. Ann became the most popular dressmaker in Tampa within a few years. Her success was due to repeat customers. Women remembered the quality of Ann's work and would call on her for future social events.

The bride-to-be loved her wedding gowns because they provided an elegant look that left women "breathless at their marvelous beauty." In 1927, the *Social Mirror* claimed, "There have been very few big weddings in the last years that Ann Cone West did not have the responsibility of the gowns worn by the bride and her attendants." No other dressmaker during this time could match Ann's designs. Her couture dresses were exclusive and very labor-intensive, which her customers loved.

Needing more space, Ann moved out of her old location in Tampa and built a large workroom behind her home. She hired well-trained helpers to keep up with the high in-demand orders. Each helper had to meet Ann's particular skill requirements. She was a passionate perfectionist when designing, and she expected the same type of energy from her workers.

The Tampa Tribune noted that Ann was very skilled at working without patterns and that much of her work "required hand stitching literally thousands of beads and sequins into intricate forms." Some clients brought their fabric to Ann's shop. Although Ann did not appear to work from patterns, she did maintain a client record "of their sizes and any physical irregularities such as minute differences of shoulder height-on file." Ann did not repeat designs, a tradition that began in Tampa and continued throughout her career.

Ann proudly recalled in a 1976 interview with the Tampa Tribune, "You know, I never made two dresses alike, except for bridesmaids' dresses. After making a debutante or wedding dress, I filed the sketch away with swatches of the material. It was never used again. My customers really loved that." Former customers recalled that they would go to Ann's shop the evening of their events and slip into their gowns right at her shop. "I would dress at her shop…and sail into the night. There was never any question of fit, and there never were any complications about it, said one loyal customer.

While most of Ann's clients were white, she always felt a tremendous responsibility to share her success with black women in her community. Ann offered dressmaking classes to a small group of neighborhood women on her days off. A black woman named Martha Ravannah worked as a tailor for Ann in 1928.

In a 1965 Tampa Tribune article, Ravannah described the working environment at *Annie's Dresses*: "The studio had three dress forms, a long cutting table, a cabinet for accessories…and a few sewing machines." It was reported that Ann employed at least eighteen women and the "Annie Cone West" brand became the launching pad for several of Tampa's African American seamstresses. Being associated with Annie Cone West was helpful in the world of Tampa's society dressmakers since Ann's customers were the only white group of women from Tampa's high society.

Ann's solid customer base brought her enormous success, but financial responsibilities that Ann was not business savvy enough to handle came with that success. She didn't know how to budget the money she was making from her shop or how much she should charge for her designs to make a profit. Ann's primary concern was making beautiful dresses and not worrying about money. The money earned from the family's dressmaking business back in Montgomery was handled by her sister Sallie, who tried to show Ann how to manage cash and inventory, but Ann's focus remained on designing. "My great-grandmother showed no interest in handling the financial side of her business," said great-granddaughter Linda. This neglect of financial management would hurt Ann's professional career for the rest of her life.

Along with financial issues, Ann also faced severe business challenges posed by the social conditions of the time. Tampa was racially segregated like all southern communities in the early twentieth century. Businesses and facilities were officially segregated in 1905, but the people of Tampa lived in divided societies long before official laws were established.

Ann's white competitors maintained a significant advantage over her because there were no physical, legal, or social reasons to separate them from their customers. Many white property owners did not rent to black dressmakers, but white dressmakers could easily rent workspace in the middle of Tampa's central business

district. White supply vendors rarely did business with black business owners, and if they did business with them, they marked up their prices for the black consumer. Regardless of her husband's advice not to work with some white vendors, Ann worked with them anyway, often paying much more than what the materials and supplies were worth. Ann ran a successful business in Tampa for years despite the racial climate.

# Chapter Eight

# THE GASPARILLA BALL

***"I remember something my mother once told me that no dream is too big or too small for God to fulfill." – Ann Lowe***

In 1926, Mrs. Lee met with the Gasparilla Festival committee to recommend Ann as the primary designer to create the gowns for the upcoming Gasparilla Ball. The elaborate ball followed a weeklong celebration with parades, live music, and activities for the whole family. The festival featured the junior members of Tampa's society as members of royalty for the festival's length. Ann saw this as an opportunity to broaden her brand beyond Tampa. Ann was commissioned to create several delicate gowns for the attendees of the coronation ball.

One of the gowns Ann designed was a beautiful flapper-style dress for the 1926 Gasparilla Ball. "The asymmetrical neckline has one jeweled shoulder strap," Margaret Powell writes. "A large, jeweled medallion in the upper left of the bodice and a series of small medallions towards the bottom of the skirt are connected with sprays

of brilliants…in a pattern reminiscent of tree branches or curling smoke. Each tiny bead was attached individually." The gowns Ann designed for Gasparilla were an enormous success. Women all over Tampa raved about her designs. "If you didn't have a Gasparilla gown by Annie," a Tampa resident recalled in 1965, "you might as well stay home." The "Annie Cone West" dress shop was responsible for dozens of dresses worn at Gasparilla in 1926.

The feeling of success did not outweigh Ann's sadness of not being allowed to attend the "Whites Only" Gasparilla Ball. With tears in her eyes, she spoke with a reporter from the Tampa Bay Times in 1968 about how it made her feel being excluded from the event because of the color of her skin, "I couldn't understand how my gowns could be accepted, but I wasn't, or how people could praise me in private, but deny me in public. It really hurt me," said Ann.

Even with the success of the Gasparilla Ball, Ann felt she had reached a plateau in Tampa. She no longer thought she could grow artistically or professionally in Tampa. She expressed her frustrations to Mrs. Lee that the social constraints of Tampa and the Jim Crow laws made it impossible for her to advance the way she wanted to. Ann was grateful for the opportunities Tampa afforded her, and although she had flourished in Tampa for years, it was now Tampa that was hindering her. After hearing her concerns, Mrs. Lee strongly agreed with Ann that she had outgrown Tampa and was "too good to waste herself" in a small southern town.

So, with no business contacts or family members living in New York, Ann and Caleb moved their family to New York. In a 1968 article with the Tampa Bay Times, Ann talked about taking the gigantic leap of faith to New York, "I questioned whether or not I was doing the right thing. I thought maybe I was dreaming too big. Then I remembered something my mother once told me: no dream is too big or small for God to fulfill. God always has a way of bringing things back again when you least expect it," said Ann.

# Chapter Nine

# A NEW LIFE IN NEW YORK

***"Leaving your comfort zone is the hardest thing to do, but it's the best thing to do."– Ann Lowe***

A week before Ann moved to New York, Mrs. Lee was invited to a party in New York City. Mrs. Lee showed up at the party wearing a hand-painted floral motif gown designed by Ann. Several New York socialites attending the event admired Mrs. Lee's dress so much that they flooded her with many questions about who had made the stunning gown. The women insisted that Ann be brought to New York to spruce up their wardrobes by the end of the evening.

So, with a few potential connections from Mrs. Lee, Ann was further convinced that New York was the place she should be. When Ann's clients in Tampa found out that she was leaving, there was much sadness. Before Ann left for New York, a Tampa socialite spoke with The Social Mirror newspaper in Tampa on the vast impact

Ann's dresses had on her and the ladies in Tampa, "If you didn't have one of Ann's gowns, you might as well have stayed home," she said.

The Social Mirror article also mentioned Ann's new career move, "There is much 'weeping and wailing and maybe gnashing of teeth.' To use the old expression, among Tampa society maids over the fact that Ann Cone West is going to New York City. Tampa society is wondering just how it will be able to survive the future social seasons without her assistance." Those who knew Ann well said the article delighted her. It was the perfect ending to a successful run.

In 1928, Ann, her husband Caleb, son Arthur, two of Ann's assistants, Ruth Williams Alexander, Ann's adopted daughter, and Tommie Mae Cole, a cousin from Montgomery, moved to New York with $20,000, a small fortune back in 1928. Half of the money came from Ann and Caleb's savings fund, while they borrowed the other half from two prominent families in Tampa.

They rented a small studio apartment, which Ann also used as a workspace. Once she got settled, she was eager to connect with Mrs. Lee's contacts. Ann expected Mrs. Lee's New York contacts to buy dresses from her and secure "a suitable location…for a modiste shop" that Ann would "have entire charge of."

As described by the Saturday Evening Post article, the reality of the situation may have been less than ideal. "Like in Tampa, Miss Lowe

called a large workroom in Harlem *Annie's Dresses.* Miss Lowe rented a third-floor workroom and living quarters on West 46th Street and limped along for a year, making few dresses. Then her money ran out," the article stated.

The cost of running her business in New York was high, and Ann was, in no way, accustomed to the expenses her new business required. *Sepia* magazine reported Ann didn't realize that her company was losing money until the end of that first year. Looking back on the situation, Ann admitted that she "devoted too little attention to economic matters and concentrated on the work itself." Like before, in Montgomery and Tampa, managing money will prove an ongoing problem for Ann.

# Chapter Ten

# A WHOLE NEW WORLD

***"You know it's time to start something new when you can feel the possibilities deep down inside."*** *– Ann Lowe*

When Ann arrived in New York City in 1928, the city was electrifying. In an article with The Amsterdam News in 1962, Ann shared her feelings about returning to New York in 1928. "I couldn't believe the energy I felt when I came back to New York. It was so freeing and refreshing. I immediately felt at ease. I was very hopeful that I could make it in New York," said Ann.

During this time, the Harlem Renaissance, an artistic African American cultural movement of the 1920s and 1930s, was in full swing. The Harlem Renaissance celebrated African American art, literature, music, and fashion. It attracted black writers, artists, musicians, photographers, poets, scholars, and fashion designers from different parts of the country. Because of this newfound cultural awareness, the "black entrepreneur" was on the rise in

Harlem. More black people owned their own homes and businesses and attended college more than any other time in America. It was an exciting time for African Americans, and Ann felt blessed to be a part of this movement.

It was also a place where creative black people came to indulge in the rich African American cultural scene called the Harlem Renaissance. It's understandable why so many Black people flocked to New York in hopes of a better way of life.

Since Harlem was the happening spot for Black people, Ann wanted to be right in the middle of all the action. Luckily for her, she found a lovely apartment in the heart of Harlem, and it didn't take long for Caleb to find a job as a doorman at an upscale hotel. Ann and Caleb enjoyed the fast-paced life of Harlem and its thriving nightlife. They enjoyed going to clubs where artistic people like Duke Ellington, Langston Hughes, Billie Holiday, James Baldwin, Sarah Vaughn, Cab Calloway, Louis Armstrong, Zora Neale Hurston, Myles Davies, Ella Fitzgerald, and Ralph Ellison attended.

While dining out frequently, Ann noticed that the women in New Yorker didn't dress like the women back in Tampa. In New York, women's fashion was much chicer, hipper, and less restricting than Ann's fashion in Tampa. That could be because New Yorkers were looking up to Paris for fashion trends. The chemise (French for shirt)

type dress, which hung straight down to the knees, was very popular in 1928.

The flapper dress and several other clothing styles were equally popular. Sleek, curveless dresses were worn with bust flattening bras. The waist completely disappeared, and belts were worn around the hips. Skirt lengths fluctuated, women donned flashy evening attire, comfortable sportswear, conservative work suits, and dresses hung straight or flared at the hip. But despite the variety, women's fashion in 1928 broke free of the physical and social constraints of the previous decade.

The clothing seen in the African American community was constantly changing and developing. The old prim and proper styles were slowly replaced with sleek and swankier. During the Harlem Renaissance era, many black women preferred short skirts, silk stockings, drop-waisted dresses, and cloche hats. Although performing in Paris during the height of the Harlem Renaissance, Dancer Josephine Baker was also a significant fashion trendsetter for black and white women alike. Women copied her style but, of course, with less revealing dresses. Men were also updating their wardrobes as well.

They were replacing their structure-forming suits for looser fitting suits called "Zoot Suits." These suits consist of wide-legged, high-waisted, peg-top trousers and a long coat with padded shoulders and

wide lapels. Men wore wide-brimmed hats, colored socks, white gloves, and velvet-collared Chesterfield coats. Also, during this time, African Americans wanted to show respect to their heritage by wearing leopard-skin coats, indicating the power of the African animal.

It took some time before Ann fully embraced this new style of fashion. She wasn't quite ready to give up on designing big ball gowns and formal dresses, a technique she loved, which made her successful. Ann faced a problem: could she find a solid customer base for her type of designs in New York? And if she could, would it be enough to run a successful business? It seemed like an uphill battle to get customers during the earlier months of starting her business. "No one flocked in," Ann told the *Daily News* in 1965. "I kept afloat for a whole year making the wedding gown and trousseau for Carlotta Cuesta"—a former Gasparilla queen," said Ann.

This Cuesta commission was the break Ann needed to secure more work. People were interested in knowing who designed the bride's wedding dress at the wedding; before long, word spread of Ann's exceptional dressmaking skills. "Every new customer, fabric vendor, and professional relationship needed to be cultivated from scratch, and for all intents and purposes, the designer who had completed hundreds of professional garments for elite members of Tampa society had to start over. Slowly, she began to build an

impressive clientele of women from New York's wealthiest families," said historian Margaret Powell.

Ann later told a reporter from the *Oakland Tribune* in 1966, "I just knew that I could come to New York and make fabulous dresses for a society of people and that one day my gowns would be worn by many." Her family felt the same way about Ann's gift for creating spectacular gowns. Her cousin, Lewis Cole, explained, "Ann just had a special gift that set her apart. It was like a miracle gift. She could see a gown in her mind and make it." Ann's gift of design would have to carry her and her family through one of the darkest times in American History.

## Chapter Eleven

# FINDING THE WAY

***"I focus my attention on not fighting the old but building on the new." – Ann Lowe***

Ann's first year in New York was financially and personally challenging. While building her business, she struggled to be a good wife and mother. After a year of working, Ann finally got her bearings when the New York stock market crashed suddenly. The Stock Market Crash began on October 24, 1929, and is reported to be the most devastating Stock market crash in the history of United States. People were losing their jobs, savings, homes, and even taking their own lives. Countless businesses were forced to close during this time.

Major fashion houses like Hattie Carnegie and department stores like Saks Fifth Avenue were not immune to the financial distress of the day. Still, they also had the capital and established clientele to remain in business. Smaller businesses had smaller financial cushions. The least established designers like Ann and many others

in New York had the most to lose. Their clients, the wives, and daughters of bankers and business owners, were no longer in the market for couture wardrobes. Some designers, like Elizabeth Hawes, stayed afloat in their shops by reducing staff salaries dramatically and offering clothing to existing clients for whatever they could pay.

Designers gave up their showrooms and workspaces and sought any work they could find through the large fashion houses of the Garment District. Ann recalled in *Sepia* magazine that she was always turned down when looking for a job until she discovered why. "I would ask shop owners for just a place to work and some fabric. I even offered to make the dresses for nothing, and you only pay me if they sell. I was constantly turned down. I waited to see if white seamstresses were being turned down one time. It didn't surprise me that after an owner told me no, minutes later, a white seamstress was told yes," said Ann.

Ann relied on Caleb, who found odd jobs to support the family during this time. After months of having design shops reject her offer to design for low pay, an unnamed shop owner finally accepted her request, and Ann was back to creating her designs. Ann recalled how her first gown sold immediately and that many others followed. The success of this arrangement allowed Ann to create similar working relationships with several established design houses throughout the great depression years. Some places did not pay her

for what her gowns were worth, and a few of them took credit for her designs. Unfortunately, Ann had to work under these circumstances to pay her bills, but she never forgot the humiliation.

During this period, she worked a great deal for established houses such as Hattie Carnegie and Chez Sonia (owned by Sonia Levienne). These arrangements allowed her to stay busy when many independent dressmakers were without work. Ann's income was probably not comparable to her money during her years in Florida. Still, she was working and able to keep her apartment in a fashionable section of Harlem. Everyone in Ann's household, including her two assistants, did their part to chip in.

And when Ann's career was on hold, she and her assistants continued to work as dressmakers for other design houses. However, Ann had to find an equivalent to the large annual business she experienced in Tampa to earn a substantial profit. She would need to secure steady work and the right connections to pursue her dreams of opening and running a successful dress shop in New York.

An excellent connection for Ann was about to walk into her life. While Ann was working at a dress shop on Manhattan Ave, a New York socialite named Polly Bush came to the shop. Bush fell in love with a gown that Ann had designed. Bush was blown away by how elegant Ann's dresses were and felt Ann "was too good to be hidden away here." Bush believed in Ann's designs so much that she

promised to introduce Ann "to the right people," and she did. The Bush connection helped shift Ann's career from stalled to putting her dresses on the fast track in New York's predominantly white fashion industry. Ann was about to step into a whole new world.

# Chapter Twelve

# READY FOR A COMEBACK

***"I don't care how many times I heard no; I always came back for that one yes." – Ann Lowe***

With Bush's help, Ann secured exclusive commissions to design for some of the most socially prominent families of the New York Social Register. Ann was on her way to establishing herself in New York as a leader in extraordinary wedding gowns and debutante dresses. Although money was still tight in America because of the stock market crash, many wealthy families still had money to spend on entertainment and fashion. Ann quickly found herself in high demand to design dresses for social events with word-of-mouth recommendations. With the help of her assistants, Ann fulfilled numerous dress orders, which provided a lucrative stream of income for her and her assistants. The debut season would become an excellent and reliable

part of Ann's business. She made the bulk of her money from designing debutante dresses. The *Saturday Evening Post* described the new craze as the "Debutante Whirl."

With the economy picking back up from the stock market crash, Ann was ready to open a dress shop, but before she could do so, she had to deal with the harsh reality of racism. According to historian Margaret Powell, "In 1930, when Ann was looking for space to open a new shop in New York, she had to take a white person with her because black people could not rent commercial property in upscale neighborhoods. In New York." On September 21, 1930, with the help of Ann's old client and good friend, Polly Bush, and just two years after moving to New York, Ann reopened *Annie's Dresses* in a small boutique in Harlem.

Ann's career was finally promising; unfortunately, her marriage was not. In an interview with *Ebony* magazine, Ann described the toll the demands of her work took on her family and why her second marriage failed. "My second husband left me. He said he wanted a 'real wife,' not one who was forever jumping out of bed to stretch dresses," said Ann. After they divorced, Caleb moved to Connecticut while Ann remained in New York with her son. She never married again. Ann used her maiden name, Lowe, as a professional decision and a personal one.

No matter what kind of storm was raging in Ann's life, she remained resilient. Like when a few fashion houses she worked for took advantage of her by attaching their labels to her designs and pocketing most of her profits, Ann didn't just sit by and do nothing. When the tiny 4'11, 98-pound woman would boldly confront the owners of these fashion houses, they would insist that they did nothing improper. "There wasn't much my great-grandmother could do back then. She was a black woman with basically no rights. I'm sure if she complained too much, she would have been "blackballed" or deemed a "troublemaker" within the fashion industry. So even if she was angry, she never let her anger show. She played with the hand that was dealt with her to keep her career," said great-granddaughter Linda.

"I can remember her telling me that she had to deal with being called the n-word by merchants at a particular fashion house while other white co-workers looked on. One woman spat on her at a fashion show when the woman found out my great-grandmother was the designer of a dress she liked. She told my great-grandmother that she would rather be dead than wear anything from a "nigger gal." In one incident, she ordered some fabric from a store, and when she went to pick it up, she noticed that the material smelled like urine. When she confronted the sales clerk, all they did was laugh. She tried to tell the store manager what happened, and he told her either to buy the material as it was or to call the police on her, claiming she

was disturbing the peace. These are the types of humiliation she had to endure. So, it's understandable why she wouldn't question any person in authority out of fear for her life," said great-granddaughter Linda.

Ann knew as a black woman in white America that she was to be seen and not heard. She had lived long enough to know that she had to tread lightly and be extremely careful not to accuse or even insinuate that a white person was mistreating her. Ann was fired the last time she accused a white shop owner of cheating her out of some money, so she had to be extremely careful. Ann spoke to *Ebony* in 1966 about how this made her feel. "I felt helpless and used. I knew many of those fashion houses were taking advantage of me, but I couldn't afford a lawyer to prove it, and even if I could, there was no way a colored woman would win against any white person," said Ann. Throughout Ann's career, she would experience other designers taking credit for her designs, causing her to lose substantial income and recognition for her work. Each betrayal would cut more profound than the last.

# Chapter Thirteen

# BUILDING A BRAND

***"When people hear the name Ann Lowe, I hope they think of excellence." – Ann Lowe***

From 1930 to 1940, Ann designed dresses for a few fashion houses while also operating her shop. In 1941, Ann was commissioned through a high-end fashion house to create a beautiful wedding dress for one of New York's most prominent socialite women, Jane Tanner Trimingham. The couture wedding gown is significant because it is one of the earliest garments with an "Ann Lowe" label. The couture wedding gown was made from artificial silk. It featured a stunning silhouette with embellished trapunto lilies, dewy with seed pearls, cascade down the bodice, and satin bubbles trimmed the hem.

In a 1981 interview, Mrs. Trimingham remembered that the use of Bermuda Lilies, placed on the neckline and the sleeves, was her idea and that Ann executed it with great skill. The gown also featured a twenty-foot train. This gown is considered to be one of Ann's

favorites. The dress is now preserved at the Met Costume Institute. The wedding gown was an immense success for the fashion house Ann designed it for.

By the mid-1940s, Ann continued to work for other fashion houses while still operating her shop. Ann was looking for new ways to expand her clientele and advertise her business. She thought a great way to do that was to attend New York's Fashion Week in 1946. The first New York fashion week started in 1943 by Eleanor Lambert, press director of the American fashion industry's first promotional organization, the New York Dress Institute. New York City was the first city to organize fashion shows seasonally. However, the very concept of "fashion week" originated in France.

Like all events held in the United States during the 1940s, Fashion Week was for "whites only." But that didn't stop Ann from trying to go; it only motivated her. She attended the 7-day event by pretending to be part of the cooking staff. "My great-grandmother told me that she would sneak inside the showroom and watch the festivities from a small corner in the back of the room. She was very discreet, never drawing attention to herself for fear of being thrown out of the event," said great-granddaughter Linda.

The room was filled with reporters from top fashion magazines and mainstream newspaper outlets. All the models were wearing elegant clothes from some of the best designers. An interview with Sepia in

1956 reveals what Ann thought, seeing all those beautiful clothes. "I felt like I had died and gone to designer heaven. Seeing all those beautiful gowns made me want to do better with my designs," said Ann. Ann spotted a designer she had admired during one particular fashion show. Eager to meet her, Ann took off the white service jacket she used to disguise herself as a member of the cooking staff to reveal a beautiful blue dress that she had designed herself. She topped off her outfit with her signature hat and chic round-framed glasses.

Ann gathered up enough courage to approach designer Sonia Rosenberg. Years later, Ann explained the encounter with Rosenberg to Sepia magazine, "I could tell she was a little surprised that a negro woman was approaching her. I told her that I was a designer with my shop, but I was interested in freelancing with her shop. Honey, she looked me up and down and saw the dress I was wearing, so I guess she believed me because she told me to drop by her shop the following day to see about possibly working together," said Ann.

Ann's great-granddaughter Linda shares her thoughts on Ann's decision to collaborate with Sonia Rosenberg, "My great-grandmother liked working independently, so it was surprising that she wanted to work with or work for another designer. But even with my great-grandmother's steady clientele, she still wanted to expand her brand. You must remember; she didn't have the same type of

support behind her as white designers did. So, she had to find ways to get more exposure, and working with an established designer like Sonia Rosenberg at the time, would have helped her achieve that," said great-granddaughter Linda.

Within a week, Ann began working at Sonia Gowns, Inc. The working relationship between Ann and Sonia appeared to be a cordial one, but Ann stayed cautious because of past betrayals. She reminded herself that working with Sonia was a way to build up her clientele and gain more mainstream media attention, not to become best friends. Ann worked part-time for Sonia, then she would go home and sew for her notable clients. Ann's grueling pace was hard, and within six months, she knew she couldn't keep up the hectic pace much longer. Fortunately, she didn't have to worry about providing childcare for Arthur because he was a grown man working as an assistant tailor at a Harlem dry cleaner.

Ann prayed for a breakthrough, and it finally happened when a young, beautiful actress named Olivia de Havilland walked into Sonia's Gowns looking for a dress to wear to the 19th Annual Academy Awards ceremony. Ann knew who Olivia was and was excited about the possibility of her picking one of her gowns to wear. She knew if Olivia picked one of her gowns, the publicity could change her life. After looking through over twenty gowns, Olivia fell in love with a dress designed by Ann. She chose a strapless tulle gown with a vibrant, hand-painted, sequined floral motif.

On March 13, 1947, Olivia de Havilland won an Oscar for Best Actress for her To Each His performance. When Olivia won the Academy Award, her dress appeared in countless newspapers and magazines throughout the country and worldwide. Ann felt this was the break she needed to compel her to the fashion designer status she worked hard to achieve. Unfortunately, Ann's hopes were shattered when she found out that Sonia told media outlets that she was the designer of Olivia's gown. All media accounts credited Olivia de Havilland's gown to the head of Sonia Gowns, Sonia Rosenberg.

Ann was furious. She confronted Sonia and asked her to tell the press that it was her design. When Sonia refused to do so, Ann ended their working relationship. Olivia de Havilland's gown was the most well-known Ann Lowe original gown until this point, and it's so unfortunate that she didn't receive credit for her work.

The *Saturday Evening Post* reported the gown was featured in Vogue, with the editorial copy, "Only Sonia could design a dress like this one." The betrayal left Ann mentally exhausted. Once sure of her purpose, she now questioned it. She believed God had called her a fashion designer, but it seemed like everything was working against her. "The situation with Sonia Rosenberg was tough on my great-grandmother. According to my mother, my great-grandmother went through a brief depression," said great-granddaughter Linda.

# Chapter Fourteen

# KNOWING YOUR WORTH

***"It took me a long time to know the difference between what I was getting and what I deserve." – Ann Lowe***

After working for Sonia Inc., Ann continued to work for different fashion houses while maintaining her dress shop. When business was slow, she made clothes for her neighbors and church members—charging them little to nothing. It was never about fame or making a lot of money with Ann. Like most designers, she simply wanted to make women feel beautiful and receive credit for her designs.

When Ann would see women wearing her dresses in New York City, she would often walk up to them and let them know she was their dress designer. According to her great-granddaughter Linda, this didn't always go over so well, "Once, my great-grandmother walked up to a white woman in New York wearing one of her dresses and told the woman that she was happy that she was wearing one of her designs; the woman called her a liar because the label sewn on the

dress was that of a white designer. I believed that's one of the reasons why many magazine editors were not asking my great-grandmother about her work because they simply didn't know it was her work," said great-granddaughter Linda.

While working at a famous fashion house, Ann walked over to the warehouse where the finished garments were distributed to different stores. Ann learned firsthand that workers would put another designer's label on her dresses before her dresses were distributed from the warehouse instead of hers. Vowing to put her name on her dresses, Ann made friends with a black seamstress named Wilma Harrison, whose job was to sew the designers' labels on the finished garments. Ann felt Wilma was the answer to her problem.

In a 1972 interview with *Sepia* magazine, Wilma shared her first meeting with Ann, "I didn't know a black woman worked as a dressmaker at the fashion house until Annie walked into the warehouse. She was upset her name was not on her dresses, so we replaced the fashion houses' labels with an "Ann Lowe" label, so customers knew their clothing. This went on for a couple of months before someone figured out what we were doing. Of course, we were fired, but I never considered getting fired as something bad. I felt it was important to stand up for yourself and not let anyone take what is yours, you know," said Wilma Harrison. After this experience, Ann and Wilma found work at different fashion houses and remained friends for the rest of their lives.

# Chapter Fifteen

# I'LL SEE YOU IN PARIS

***"The next thing I knew, I was having high tea with Christian Dior at the Hotel Ritz in Paris."– Ann Lowe***

A chance meeting in 1947 with an editor from a prominent black newspaper outlet presented Ann with an opportunity of a lifetime. Ann always dreamed about going to Paris, but she didn't think she would ever have the chance of going until a leading African American publication called *The New York Age*, a black newspaper produced from 1887 to 1960, contacted her. The newspaper was one of the most influential black newspapers of its time. After returning from Paris, Ann wrote an occasional fashion column for *The New York Age*.

They were familiar with Ann's designs and felt she would be an excellent choice to go to Paris on their behalf and report on the Paris Fashion Week. The 1947 Paris Fashion week introduced a new French designer named Christian Dior, featuring his first

collection: *Corolle*. The first recognized Paris Fashion Week was held in October 1973.

"*The New York Age* spent a lot of money to send Ann to Paris in style. She stayed at the luxurious Hôtel Lutétia while covering the postwar couture shows. Ann felt at home in Paris. She enjoyed visiting all the historical sites in Paris: The Louvre, the Eiffel Tower, and the famous fashion houses of Paris. Ann was a long way from her humble beginnings in Montgomery, Alabama. As she walked through the streets of Paris, she thought about her family and how proud her mother and grandmother would be of her.

The fashions and the historical sites weren't the only things Ann enjoyed in Paris; she also enjoyed the exciting black nightlife Paris offered. During this time, Paris was experiencing a fast-growing African American community in the aftermath of World War II, when about 200,000 black people were brought to fight. Ninety percent of these soldiers were from the American South. After being well received by the French, most black GIs stayed in France, and other blacks followed them. Many black people viewed France as a welcome change from the widespread racism in the United States. During this time, jazz got introduced to the French, and shortly after, black culture was born in Paris. Black musicians, artists, designers, actors, and Harlem Renaissance writers found Paris ready to embrace them with open arms. Decades later, African Americans still settled in Paris because of its rich culture and classic fashions.

Not only was Ann in Paris to report on fashion week, but she was also in Paris to promote the "Ann Lowe" brand. Every day during fashion week, Ann made sure she advertised her designs the best way she knew how, and that was to wear them. Women would stop her on the streets of Paris and ask her, "Who are you wearing?" That question always flattered Ann, for she knew the answer would always be an "Ann Lowe Original." Her 4'11", 98-pound frame was always dressed to perfection, worthy of a first-class fashion designer.

Ann found Paris fashion to be posher and non-traditional than New York dresses, especially the dresses she made for high society clients like Marjorie Merriweather Post, sole heiress to the Post Cereal fortune, who was also in Paris at the same time as Ann. The two ladies were happy to see each other. Ann proudly recalled an incident in Paris when she and Marjorie Post attended the same fashion show.

Ann was speechless to watch Marjorie Post introduce her to acquaintances around the room as "Miss Lowe, head of the American House of Ann Lowe." Notably, someone of Marjorie Post's social status would feel comfortable introducing her African American dress designer around a fashion house in Paris to suggest that Ann's work was of the same quality as French designers. Ann recounted this story in several interviews and was amused by the encounter.

"Marjorie Post had many occasions to wear formal clothes, and while she purchased gowns from a wide range of high-quality stores and designers such as Saks Fifth Avenue and Hattie Carnegie, her patronage of Ann's work is representative of the interest socialites of all ages held for Ann Lowe Originals throughout the major metropolitan centers of the East Coast. This incident also suggests a warm working relationship between the two women," said historian Margaret Powell.

Marjorie Post was also kind enough to introduce Ann to fashion designer Christian Dior. Ann admired Dior's work and was thrilled to meet him. According to fashion historians, when Dior met Ann for the first time, he admired while examining the craftsmanship of her dress so much that he immediately wanted to know: "Who made this gown?" When Ann replied she made the dress, Dior complimented her on "her competent artistry."

The two got along very well. Ann and Christian met for high tea twice in Paris. He wanted to know about New York fashions while she wanted to learn about Paris fashions. Before leaving Paris, Dior gave Ann one of his first signature handbags. According to Ann's great-granddaughter Linda, "That handbag was one of the few fashion accessories that my great-grandmother truly cherished."

# Chapter Sixteen

# DRESSING AMERICAN ROYALTY

***"Sometimes I pinch myself when I think about all the famous women who have worn my designs." – Ann Lowe***

When Ann returned to New York from Paris, things were turning around for America's economy. The post-war years were here, and it was a prosperous time. The wealthy returned to the opera, the ballet, the theater, debutante balls, and formal events. Women who could afford these events were shopping around for evening gowns, and Ann was ready to dress them.

Inspired by Parisian fashion, Ann couldn't wait to start designing again. Thanks to her relationship with Marjorie Post, Ann picked up new clients while maintaining her already steady clients. Within a few months of returning from Paris, Ann began designing dresses for women who belonged to some of the wealthiest families in New

York. Her socialite clients included the Rockefellers, the Duponts, the Whitneys, the Vanderbilts, and the Rothschilds.

In 1950, Ann and her grown son Arthur opened a more prominent boutique, *Ann Lowe's Gowns*, at 973 Lexington Avenue. New York's elites were flocking to her new, upscale store, which gave her the financial stability she needed. New clients like socialites Jacqueline and Lee Bouvier and their mother, Janet Auchincloss, became frequent customers. Ann designed many party dresses for the Bouvier sisters, including their 1947 debut gowns. Still, it would be the wedding of one of the Bouvier sisters that will forever cement Ann Lowe's fashion legacy. We'll come back to that a little later.

The pieces of Ann's career were starting to align with the dreams she had dreamt for herself back in Montgomery, Alabama; to be a great designer. Ann talked about her love for dressmaking in an article for *Ebony*, "I feel so happy when I am making clothes that I could just jump up and down with joy. There is nothing sweeter than me sitting at my desk with a sketch pad or hearing the sound of my sewing machine," said Ann. What also made her equally happy was having her son Arthur, now 38, join her business by keeping the shop's books and ordering her materials.

Ann was ready to take on more intricate designs and loved a good artistic challenge. One of those creative challenges came in June 1953, when Ann received a phone call from New York socialite,

Janet Auchincloss, requesting to meet with her. Ann didn't find this request unusual because she had designed dresses for Mrs. Auchincloss and her daughters. When Mrs. Auchincloss showed up at Ann's shop, she arrived with a beautiful young woman by her side. That young woman was her daughter, Jacqueline (Jackie) Bouvier.

Ann was delighted when she learned Jackie was engaged to be married to a young Senator named Jack Kennedy, and she wanted Ann to design her wedding dress. Ann's excitement quickly turned to panic when she learned she would only have four months to create Jackie's wedding dress, Mrs. Auchincloss' mother-of-the-bride dress (which Mrs. Auchincloss wore for both of her daughters' weddings), and twelve bridesmaids' dresses. Mrs. Auchincloss assured Ann that she would do a fabulous job designing the dresses for what was being called the "wedding of the century." Okay, no pressure there.

Ann was feeling a great deal of pressure from designing something exceptional. She relied on Jackie to help navigate her through the process. While Jackie tried to take the reins of her coming wedding day, the patriarch of the Kennedy family, Joseph Kennedy, Sr., was calling all the shouts. Kennedy historians suggest that Mr. Kennedy was in control of every detail of the massive wedding, including the confidentiality agreement he had Ann sign.

Few people knew Ann had to sign a confidentiality agreement form before designing the bridal party dresses. "I'm sure my great-grandmother didn't know much about confidentiality agreements, but Mr. Kennedy felt that his son, John Kennedy, was already an important member of the U.S. Senate. Perhaps, he might run for president one day, so she needed not to try to trade upon the Kennedy name for recognition. But none of that confidentiality stuff mattered to my great-grandmother. She was just happy to be collaborating with the Auchincloss family once again," said great-granddaughter Linda.

With any bride, it's always essential for her to meet several times with the designer of her dress, and Jackie was no exception. Ann asked Jackie what type of wedding dress she envisioned at the early sketch meetings described in the Saturday Evening Post. Jackie, who had just returned from Paris, said she wanted something simple, chic, and French, resembling Parisian fashion. After meeting a few times, Ann presented Jackie with sketches of what she envisioned for her wedding dress, and Jackie happily approved the drawings.

However, according to Kennedy historians, Jackie's future father-in-law wasn't entirely on board with Jackie's vision. Joseph Kennedy, Sr., thought Jackie's gown could send the wrong message to America with a dress that seemed to idolize "foreign glamour." Ann told a reporter in an article with the *Saturday Evening Post,* "I believe Mr. Joseph Kennedy, Sr. wanted Jackie's wedding dress to

be an elegant fairytale ball gown, but Jackie had envisioned something different. She wanted to use her Grandmother Lee's long, expansive rose point Irish lace mantilla paired with a sleek, elegant gown," said Ann. Jackie used her grandmother's lace for her veil, but she didn't get the type of dress she wanted.

Once Ann received approval on all sketches, she and her six assistants began working on this large order. Ann and her assistants worked long, hard hours to complete the intricate designs of each dress. After a dress was finished, Ann would carefully scrutinize it to ensure it was perfect. Each hem, seam, and zipper had to meet Ann's level of perfection. If something wasn't right, she didn't care how many times it had to be fixed, as long as it was done correctly. Ann didn't play when it came to sewing. Her legendary finishing touches and care for details were what Mrs. Auchincloss loved about Ann's designs. So, Ann knew she couldn't disappoint the bride or the bride's mother; everything had to be perfect.

Making Jackie's wedding gown took eight weeks and six weeks to make the bridesmaid's dresses. It took thousands of hand stitches to construct the bridal party dresses. When all the dresses were finished, Ann proudly hand-stitched her Ann Lowe label inside each dress. Ann and her entire team were delighted with the outcome of the dresses. The long hours were finally behind them, and they could breathe a sigh of relief, or so they thought.

# Chapter Seventeen

# WHAT COULD GO WRONG?

***"You can't always control what happens to you, but you can control how you react to it."-Ann Lowe***

Unfortunately, their excitement was short-lived. Ann and her team celebrated finishing the bridal parties' dresses a week before the wedding when a disaster happened. A water pipe broke and flooded Ann's shop, destroying 10 of the 15 dresses, including the bride's elaborate wedding gown. Ann was beyond devastated when she realized what had happened.

Ann rallied her assistants together and appealed to her suppliers to provide additional materials quickly with no time to wallow in self-pity. She could get the materials, but it was expensive to rush the order. It took two full days to cut the wedding gown, but the dresses were re-created in time for the ceremony, with her entire team

working around the clock. The wedding gown, which initially took eight weeks to make, got duplicated in five days.

With new fabric and other materials needed to make the latest dresses, Ann felt she had no other choice but to use her own money, a decision her son, Arthur, tried to make her reconsider. He wanted to tell Mrs. Auchincloss what had happened in hopes she would understand and pay for the new materials, but Ann wouldn't have it. She unknowingly gave the family a great bargain, charging just $500 (approx. $4,000 today) for Jackie's entire ensemble, compared with the $1,500 price tag the dress likely would have cost from a competitor.

Unfortunately, Ann did not take the advice of her son, which caused her financial problems later down the road. Ann would charge her clients barely enough to break even throughout her career, and her commission for the Bouvier/Kennedy wedding nearly bankrupted her. The remake of the dresses had turned a $700 profit into a $2,200 loss. Ann didn't make a fuss about what was going on. She never told Jackie or her mother about the flooding at the shop. As far as she was concerned, the issue wasn't necessary.

But one issue Ann refused to be quiet about was her treatment by one of the Auchincloss staff members. Author *Rosemary E. Reed Miller* (***Threads of Time: The Fabric of History)*** shares how Ann dealt with a humiliating racial situation. Ann took an overnight train

to the Auchincloss farm in Newport, RI, to hand-deliver the dresses herself. When she arrived at the house, an employee for the Auchincloss family told Ann that she would have to use the service door in the back if she had anything to deliver. Ann was furious. She explained to the staff member that she was the wedding dress designer, but her plea went unnoticed. Ann reportedly told the staff member, "If I must use the back door, your boss will not have these dresses, and you're going to be in a lot of trouble, not me. So, do you still want me to use the backdoor? And of course, he let me in the front door," said Ann.

This commission was a very stressful one for Ann. She had to endure a lot of unforeseen circumstances that nearly destroyed everything she had worked so hard for. "From the flooding of her shop to the encounter with the Auchincloss family's servant shows you how resilient my great-grandmother was. She wasn't one to buckle under pressure or keep quiet when someone displayed racist tendencies toward her. She always said, 'you didn't have to like me, but you do have to respect me,'" said great-granddaughter Linda.

Jackie Kennedy's beautifully crafted wedding dress was made of ivory tissue silk, with a portrait neckline, fitted bodice, and a bouffant skirt embellished with bands of more than fifty yards of fabric. Her rose point lace veil, worn first by her grandmother Lee, was draped with orange blossoms. Jackie wore a diamond bracelet that was a gift from the groom. The bride carried an elegant bouquet

of white and pink gardenias with white orchids and trailing stephanotis. Many fashion critics considered Mrs. Kennedy's wedding dress a "masterpiece." The bridesmaids' dresses received a lot of praise as well.

Over the years, there have been reports that Jackie wasn't too fond of her wedding dress, which had nothing to do with Ann's designing skills but had everything to do with her father-in-law-to-be fashion choices. According to Kimberly Chrisman-Campbell, the author of the book *"The Way We Wed: A Global History of Wedding Fashion,"* Mrs. Kennedy was no fan of the dress she wore to walk down the aisle. "Even though it's a beautiful dress, it was not what she wanted, and she compared it to a lampshade," Christman-Campbell explains, "It was chosen by her father-in-law-to-be, who wanted to create an American royalty moment and set up his son as the heir to the family dynasty."

Dressmaker Mini Rhea, who designed dresses for Jackie Kennedy in the 1950s, shares the same sentiment as Christman-Campbell. "The dress couldn't have been fancier. But I had the feeling that Jackie was trying to please everyone---to dress according to everyone's idea of a bride," said Rhea. Even if Jackie wasn't a fan of her wedding dress, she wore the dress with such style and grace. Having media outlets from all over the world cover the society wedding of the season was another aspect of the wedding that Joseph

Kennedy, Sr., took charge of. Reporters disclosed every detail of the day, except the dress designer.

# Chapter Eighteen

# IT'S ALL IN A NAME

***"I couldn't understand how my gowns could be accepted, but I wasn't, or how people could praise me in private but deny me in public. I wanted the world to know that a little colored woman from Montgomery, Alabama, named Ann Lowe, made that beautiful wedding dress for Mrs. Kennedy. Millions admired her wedding dress; unfortunately, I didn't receive the same admiration."– Ann Lowe***

Although the Kennedy wedding was highly publicized and seen worldwide, Ann received nearly no credit for designing the wedding dress. This type of publicity is what designers dream of having; their work seen worldwide, and everybody knowing their name. By giving Ann proper credit for designing Mrs. Kennedy's dress, think about how much business this might have generated for her. The possibilities could have been endless for her, but the lack of recognition and publicity hurt her personally and professionally.

As *The Huffington Post* reported, when a reporter from *Ladies' Home Journal* asked Mrs. Kennedy in 1961 who was responsible for her beautiful wedding dress, she said it was made by a "colored woman dressmaker" who was "not haute couture." Ouch! Mrs. Kennedy's reported slight was upsetting to Ann. She wrote a letter to Mrs. Kennedy, hoping to convey her most profound disappointment regarding Mrs. Kennedy's hurtful comments. "My reason for writing this note is to tell you how hurt I feel," Ann wrote. "You know I have never sought publicity, but I would prefer to be referred to as 'Ann Lowe, negro designer,' because I am. Any reference to the contrary hurts me more deeply than I can perhaps make you realize."

Letitia Baldrige, Jackie Kennedy's social secretary, called Ann a few days later to assure her that the reference to "a colored woman dressmaker" hadn't been approved by Mrs. Kennedy and to convey an apology for her distress—without, however, taking responsibility for it. Ann then engaged an attorney and sought "tangible" reparation from the *Ladies' Home Journal.* The magazine never obliged.

*The Washington Post*'s Nina Hyde was the only one who gave Ann credit for designing Jackie Kennedy's wedding dress; she wrote, "… the dress was designed by a Negro, Ann Lowe." The dress became more famous than the designer in many regards, which left Ann feeling very discouraged. "I almost gave up dreaming about the

beauty in my life and thought only of suicide," she told the *Daily News* in 1953. After the wedding, Ann took a few months off from work to focus on her mental health. Ann focused on building her brand with the Kennedy wedding finally behind her. She got a much-needed break in 1955 when one of her dresses, along with her name, appeared in VOGUE magazine.

Since Ann's designs usually went uncredited in magazines, it was a big deal to finally see her name alongside one of her designs in a mainstream fashion magazine like VOGUE. Ann's name was credited in the caption for the photo, which read, "Miss Nina Auchincloss (Jackie Kennedy's stepsister) will make her debut this month at a party at Hammersmith Farms, the Newport house of her father and stepmother, Mr. and Mrs. Hugh Auchincloss…Ann Lowe made her pale pink and green tulle dress." Ann was elated to see one of her designs in print and her name. So honored by this acknowledgment, Ann proudly hung the picture on the wall of her dress shop for the world to see.

# Chapter Nineteen

# BLACK GIRL MAGIC

***"Black folks were born with the burden of having to suppress who we are for others to feel good about themselves."– Ann Lowe***

In between designing dresses, Ann also found time to do some activist work with the NAACP. At an NAACP charity event in Harlem in 1955, Ann was seated next to the great jazz legend Ella Fitzgerald. The two hit it off and became good friends. A few months later, Ella introduced Ann to her good friend, Lena Horne. Ann designed a unique gown for Lena's live performance while visiting New York. Lena adored Ann's dresses and told other black Hollywood actresses about Ann.

By 1956, Ann's gowns were worn by black women from Harlem to Hollywood. Many white mainstream media outlets only reported Ann's white clients and not her black ones. Perhaps, using an old tactic of trying to "divide and conquer" would cause tension between Ann and the black community.

Ann's great-granddaughter Linda explains, "There have been rumors that my great-grandmother didn't like to design dresses for black women or disowned her black community once she started designing for white clients. That is simply not true. It gave my great-grandmother great pleasure to design dresses for black entertainers and women from her neighborhood in Harlem. She was proud to be black, and she loved and supported her community," says great-granddaughter Linda.

Ann didn't just sit back and ignore how black people were treated in the United States; she was a strong supporter of the NAACP. According to her great-granddaughter Linda, Ann joined the NAACP when she was not allowed to use a public building to hold a fashion show in New York City because of her skin color.

"She was angry about the racism she experienced. She was appalled that black people were attending separate schools, riding in the back of public buses, drinking from separate water fountains, and eating at different restaurants. She knew firsthand how painful it was to be called the n-word when trying to use public places marked for "Whites Only, so anything she could do to help black people get equal rights, she was all for it," says Linda.

Ann's determination to fight against racism started when she was a little girl in Montgomery, Alabama. It wasn't unusual for a young Ann to witness a cross burning on a nearby neighbor's front lawn or

to be told to walk on the opposite side of the street when white people were walking by. Ann never forgot the fear she felt as a little girl walking down the segregated streets of Montgomery, and that's why she wanted to be a part of an organization like the NAACP, which was fighting against racism.

Ann sent a lot of money to help support the Montgomery bus boycott in 1955. She felt a special bond with Civil Rights Activist Rosa Parks because they were both from the south and dressmakers. Ann spent the rest of her life fighting for equal rights for the African American community.

While African Americans continued to fight for equal rights during the 1950s, Ann fought hard to remain relevant in the predominately white fashion industry. Between 1955 and 1958 may have been the peak of Ann's independent career. During this time, the "Ann Lowe" brand was associated with high-quality couture work. She took pride in only designing clothing for a select group of clients, "I'm an awful snob. I love my clothes, and I'm particular about who wears them. I sew for the families of the Social Register," Ann said in an interview with *Ebony*.

Designing for the social register was paying off for Ann. By the late 1950s, Ann's gowns finally appeared with proper credit in *Vogue*, *Vanity Fair,* and *Town and Country* magazines. She was happy about the coverage in mainstream magazines, but she took pride in

appearing in African American magazines like *Ebony, JET,* and *Sepia;* each publication gave her exclusive coverage to showcase her designs.

In 1957, the *New York Times* acknowledged Ann as an expert in fashion "who has been turning out impeccably dressed debutantes for twenty years and charges up to $500 for her custom-made evening stunners." Many young women in New York made their social debut each year in an Ann Lowe Original. Along with her custom work, wholesale designs became a part of Ann's overall business plan by the late 1950s. Ann's couture shop was flourishing so much that she hired additional staff to keep up with the high demand. Ann was finally seeing the fruits of all her hard labor.

# Chapter Twenty

# PUSHING THROUGH THE PAIN

***"I don't think one ever recovers from losing someone they love."***

***– Ann Lowe***

While Ann enjoyed her well-deserved success, she could not have foreseen the tragedy coming her way. One snowy evening in February 1958, Ann suffered her most significant loss when her beloved son, Arthur Lee, was killed in a tragic car accident. Arthur was 45 years old. He had no children.

Sixty-year-old Ann grieved hard for her beloved son, who was also her business manager, her protector, and her best friend. People who worked for Ann said she was the happiest when Arthur worked with her. Ann was once heard saying that having her son was the best thing she'd ever done. Arthur would always escort Ann to social events. She later shared with her friends, "I never went to another party, for my escort was no longer with me."

Depression was something Ann battled with throughout her life, and losing her only child sent her into a deep depression. The love of her sister, Sallie, helped her through the darkest time of her life. It was during this challenging time that Ann and Sallie became even closer. After Arthur's death, Ann didn't want to live alone. She asked Sallie, who had recently lost her husband, to stay with her for a couple of months. Those months turned into years. She and Sallie ended up sharing a Harlem apartment for over 30 years.

"My great-grandmother enjoyed having her sister live with her. The only thing Ann loved more than fashion was her son, Arthur Lee. She and Arthur were extremely close. Since my great-grandmother gave birth to Arthur when she was a teenager, their relationship was more like two best friends instead of mother and son. Arthur grew up hanging around his mother's shop, learning about different fabrics, chatting with her clients, and eventually gaining enough knowledge about the ins and outs of the fashion industry to become her business manager. He was very protective of his mother and always tried to talk her out of reducing her prices. He tried to keep her business finances, if not profitable, at least manageable. He tried to protect her from people who tried to take advantage of her kindness. He often felt that his mother didn't quite know her self-worth regarding her designs. She was a fantastic designer but not an excellent businesswoman. She was more interested in who was wearing her clothes versus how much money she was making. What

Arthur brought to my great-grandmother's professional and private life was immeasurable in her eyes, so in losing him, she lost part of herself as well," says great-granddaughter Linda.

Many black entrepreneurs ran into financial problems like Ann with no formal education or business training. With not getting any loans from white banks, many black businesses suffered. Often, black business owners just weren't sure of their worth, which was true of Ann. She charged meager prices for her designs and was often talked into lowering her costs even further. She never considered the difference between making the designs and what she should charge for them. Her struggle to separate the two would put her in a financial bind that would change her life forever.

# Chapter Twenty-One

# A SHADOW OF DEBT

***"I tell young people today; make sure you pay more attention to the financial side of your business than the creative side…I wish I did." – Ann Lowe***

While Ann was grieving for Arthur, her sister, Sallie, ran her dress shop. When Ann finally returned to work at her shop, her primary focus was reconnecting with her clients. Sallie stayed on to manage the financial side of the business but gave it up shortly after having health issues. Ann did not hire a financial advisor or bookkeeper with Arthur and Sallie gone. Maintaining her own business became too much for Ann. Within six months of returning to work, *Ann Lowe's Gowns* began showing signs of economic ruin. Financial disaster was looming just around the corner.

By 1959, Ann was in debt to the suppliers who provided her with the exquisite, hard-to-find materials she needed for Jackie Kennedy's wedding. People close to the situation suggest Ann's

debt problems began with Mrs. Kennedy's wedding and worsened over the years. In an interview with *Ebony*, Ann talked about her financial issues. "One morning, I woke up owing $10,000 to suppliers and $12,800 in back taxes. Friends at Henri Bendel and Neiman-Marcus loaned me money to stay open, but the Internal Revenue agents finally closed me up for non-payment of taxes. At my wits' end, I ran sobbing into the street; the tears wouldn't stop falling," said Ann.

And if things couldn't get any worse, glaucoma was advancing in Ann's right eye, making it harder for her to sketch and sew. "My right eye, which was heavily damaged by glaucoma, had to be removed. I had no money, and now my eyes were failing me," said Ann in *Ebony*. While Ann was in the hospital, someone paid off her debts to the I.R.S. Ann always believed Mrs. Kennedy was her anonymous benefactor. However, this claim was never proven.

Overwhelmed by the loss of her son, loss of another dress shop, and her failing eyesight, Ann took another break from the fashion world. Ann spent most of her days sitting in her apartment, grieving for Arthur. Her sister, Sallie, was a great comfort to her. Sallie worked as a seamstress to support them, while Ann focused on her mental and physical health. After a few months off, Ann returned to work as a designer for Madeline Couture, a dress shop in New York City.

Ann had only been working for Madeline for a few months when she received an offer that she couldn't refuse.

# Chapter Twenty-Two

# RISING FROM THE ASHES

***"You learn what type of fighter you are when your back is against the wall." – Ann Lowe***

In 1960, the world of fashion was changing. The sixties ushered in a new free-spirited style of clothing, filled with bright colors and short hemlines, far different from the sophisticated style that Ann was used to designing. Even as the world of fashion was changing, Ann felt there was still a market for designs. With an impressive resume filled with high society customers, a seasoned designer like Ann would not be out of business for long. All she needed was an adequate workspace and a powerful sponsor.

Historian Margret Powell shares her insight into Ann's financial situation during this time. "Ann's financial affairs prevented her from reopening her salon, but as word spread that one of New York Society's most prolific designers was out of business, a prestigious opportunity soon appeared. Saks Fifth Avenue offered a partnership in their exclusive boutique, the Adam Room, and Ann agreed to

become Saks' first Black woman head designer. The Adam Room was an established department on the fifth floor of the flagship store. It specializes in custom and ready-to-wear debutante and bridal gowns. Being the first black head designer at the Adam Room was a big deal for Ann, but it was also a big deal for the other black people who worked at the Adam Room. They saw the hiring of Ann as a sign that things were changing for black people," said Margret Powell.

Ann's great-granddaughter Linda elaborates on how Ann's position as the first black woman designer at Saks was groundbreaking and inspirational for the black employees working in service positions at Saks. "From the start, my great-grandmother understood the significance of her position at Saks. On her first day at work, the black employees applauded her when she entered the building, so she felt the enormous responsibility of representing her people with dignity. Black workers couldn't believe this black woman had a workspace in the same building they cleaned. Over time, they became like family. They watched out for her, so every week, to show her appreciation, my great-grandmother would greet the black elevator operators, janitors, and service staff with hot coffee and donuts," said great-granddaughter Linda.

Saks was also aware of Ann's presence, so to announce New York Society's beloved designer to the Saks Fifth Ave Family, the marketing team at Saks thought of a clever advertising campaign.

Margaret Powell explains, "Saks created promotional materials featuring a pen and ink portrait of Ann Lowe in profile. The creative profile read: "Saks Fifth Avenue takes pride in announcing that the Debut and Bridal Gown Collection created by Ann Lowe can now be found exclusively at The Adam Room."

Ann was excited about her new partnership with Saks, but she didn't realize the financial stress it would have on her career. Margaret Powell explains, "In the same way that Ann looked only at the beauty going into her designs, instead of the cost, she could not predict the additional financial burden represented by the Saks offer. She was released from the burden of managing the rent of a showroom and workspace. However, in exchange for that freedom, she introduced a third party into established relationships with her most lucrative clients and lowered the amount of profit she received for each gown. From the outside, the arrangement may have looked like a golden partnership, but it became a risky arrangement for an independent designer."

Ann realized this after she reviewed some invoices from the Saks accounting department. Margaret Powell clarifies, "This partnership made excellent financial sense for the department store. For the small cost of maintaining a workspace in the building on Fifth Avenue and probably providing credit backing for Ann, they received high-quality couture work with a Saks Fifth Avenue label.

Besides, a coveted list of young women from the Social Register would be perfect customers for future services. Investing in an elderly designer who was becoming increasingly frail may be an unsteady arrangement, but realistically, Saks had a trivial risk in the partnership. In their worst scenario, if the health of their head designer declined and she became unable to produce her designs, other seamstresses at Saks would be able to complete them. Ann discussed specific conditions of the Saks arrangement herself in at least one interview during the 1960s and also described by a former employee, including the fact that Ann may have been responsible for her salary. Suppose Ann agreed to cover all the expenses related to each gown and her compensation while releasing her valuable customer list to a previous competitor, all in exchange for a place to work; in that case, she was making a huge financial error."

Once again, Ann was taken advantage of by a business she thought had her best interest at heart, but the bottom line was about money. Margaret Powell further explains, "It seems that Ann's talents were being exploited, and it is difficult to believe that the decision-makers at Saks did not understand that the compensation they were offering was uneven. It is also possible that these terms were the first offer from Saks. Their lawyers were starting low and were prepared to negotiate if Ann insisted on more profitable terms. Ann most likely negotiated the clause allowing Ann to keep her private clients, but it may have been the only detail of the original offer that she sought to

change. The logistics involved in working privately with clients within her only showroom at Saks are unclear. It is not known how many people Ann employed during this period, but her business volume required multiple assistants." We know from previous articles and documents that several employees with Ann during her Saks period have been identified as her sister Sallie, her assistant Esther Provanzano and a sketcher named Andrew Koval.

Ann may have had help artistically, but she was fighting an uphill battle financially."Presumably, the Adam Room marked up the final price of Ann's gowns on display considerably, and the final prices for the gowns were probably closer to, if not actually, higher than the actual amounts of Ann's cost. There were positive aspects to the Saks partnership. With Saks as a home base, Ann could continue making the kinds of gowns she loved without compromising quality. Presumably, backed by Saks' credit, Ann could continue to purchase high-quality materials, such as silk imported from France, from the top suppliers in the city and work in a top-quality workroom with adequate staff. She was also able to raise her professional profile through the status and reputation of the Saks name," said Margaret Powell.

Having the Saks name to promote Ann's dresses helped her reach a new group of customers, but her talent kept them coming back for more. The secret to Ann's success was the exclusive nature of her designs—no two were alike—and all her gowns were handmade and

expertly fitted. She used only the finest materials, which were often difficult to obtain. Many of her dresses featured delicate handworks, such as the exquisite handmade fabric flowers she learned to make as a child and beading, embroidery, and fringe.

Since many high-society women admired and wore her stylish designs, Ann was listed in the National Social Directory, alongside her many wealthy clients. Also, in 1961, Ann was the recipient of the prestigious 'Couturier of the Year' award, making her the first black person to win the coveted award. Because of the prestigious couturier award, Ann received an exciting and unexpected offer.

# Chapter Twenty-Three

# DESIGNING FOR THE BELLE OF THE BALL

***"You know, I've made so many dresses all these years for different debutante balls, social events, and ceremonies, yet, I have never been able to attend one because they were always for 'Whites Only.'"*– Ann Lowe**

A few weeks after receiving the 'Couturier of the Year' award, a group of executives from Omaha, Nebraska, were in New York. They were in the final stages of their search for a dress designer who could successfully handle a commission for their city's most prominent cotillion, the Ak-Sar-Ben Coronation Ball (Nebraska spelled backward). They choose Ann for the job.

Ann's Saks connection was probably crucial to her being selected as the court's couturier. The Ak-Sar-Ben committee members were

proud to announce their liaison with a sophisticated New York designer like Ann. Her race did not appear to be important to the committee. It was her experience and talent that opened the door for her. The executives considered that Ann was no newcomer to custom designing for debutantes and their social register mothers. They also felt that Ann designed the debut and wedding dress for First Lady Jacqueline Kennedy.

Ann was commissioned to design thirty-three extraordinary tulle gowns with intricate silver beading. The gowns were made from French nylon tulle. Large amounts of fabric were needed for each dress, and each dress used twelve layers of cloth and several petticoats over hoops. The dresses were heavily beaded with sequins, silver bugle beads, and rhinestones. Making these couture dresses was time-consuming because every detail demanded the type of attention that an Ann Lowe gown was known for. Even though the designing process was a lot of hard work, Ann enjoyed the challenge.

Ann had a lot of ideas about what she thought the dresses should look like, and the final designs came together like pure magic. Ann's favorite design was the Queen's gown, the most lavish of all the dresses and the most expensive. Literally, hundreds of yards of white French net, most of it more delicate than the sheerest chiffon, went into the queen's gown, custom-designed for her by Ann Lowe. The dress itself comprised 12 layers of net hand-embroidered in 60

different motifs with silver and crystal bugle beads, rhinestones, pearls, and cut-crystal pendants. Ann's high level of hand beading for thirty-three gowns was an expensive design decision.

This decision would cost her dearly in the end. The Ak-Sar-Ben committee directly paid the retail price to Saks for the gowns that Saks purchased from Ann at a wholesale rate. Ann was well known for undercharging in these arrangements, and at Saks, she often sold dresses at a loss. Ann's pattern of undercharging was not exclusive to her work with Saks; one client from her private dress shop revealed this happily to the *Saturday Evening Post*. "Ms. Lowe charged seventy dollars apiece for bridesmaid dresses that should have cost at least two hundred, but that's how she is."

Like so many times before, Ann's lack of business sense proved detrimental to her business. According to inventory records, Ann lost an average of $150 on each dress she sold through Saks; the Ak-Sar-Ben order, which should have been a jewel in Ann's body of work, quickly turned into a financial nightmare.

"Undercharging for the 33 gowns in this order would create a total loss of $4,950, and the loss was likely actually greater. To make matters worse, Saks claimed that Ann was earning similar losses on her other work, which could easily explain the $9,275.06 that Saks claimed that she owed to them during her bankruptcy proceedings in 1963. Suppose she lost money with each dress order; in that case,

it is difficult to see how she was covering her living expenses, let alone the operating costs of her Adam Room salon," said Historian Margaret Powell.

Saks may have advanced money to Ann to pay staff salaries, material costs, or living expenses. So, although the Ak-Sar-Ben Ball proved to be a colossal success for Ann artistically, it was a big flop for her financially. What started as a promising collaboration between a powerhouse company and an accomplished designer turned sour.

# Chapter Twenty-Four

# FIGHTING AGAINST ALL ODDS

***"I owed everything to my mother and grandmother. I had more freedom than they ever did, and I knew it. Because of them, I was able to live a life they couldn't." – Ann Lowe***

After the Ak-Sar-Ben Ball disaster, Ann decided to leave Saks in 1962. With the bit of money she had left and the pity of a generous landlord, Ann opened a small workspace farther down 53rd street in New York City. Unfortunately, most of Ann's employees continued to work at Saks because Saks could pay more than what Ann could offer. A few employees attempted to move with Ann but returned to Saks when Ann's financial problems affected the consistency of their earnings. Only her sister, Sallie, stayed by her side.

A solid supporting staff was an absolute necessity for Ann at this point because her increasingly poor eyesight made drawing impossible and severely limited her sewing ability. "I've had to work by feel," Ann admitted in an interview with *Sepia*, "but people tell me I've done better feeling than others do seeing." Running a shop would be impossible without a staff to sketch and take up the bulk of sewing. Ann's sketcher and chief assistant remained at Saks, and Ann could not hire new and highly trained workers who could meet the challenge of a high-volume couture shop. "I couldn't fill my orders," she admitted. "And things went from bad to worse."

Ann didn't want to tell anyone that she was having problems with her left eye. Still, her attempts to continue working with a severe cataract in her only eye led to embarrassing attempts to cover up her issues. Terrified to lose her sight, she tried to bluff. "Now, here's a design I think you'll like." She would say to a customer, picking up a sketch and bringing it close to her eyes. "Oh, my goodness," she would add brightly, "Isn't that ridiculous! I'm holding this sketch upside down!" This stunt worked for a while, but eventually, Ann needed to have surgery. Two years after opening her shop, Ann's sister Sallie ran her dress shop while Ann sought medical attention. Ann had no money for eye surgery, but with the help of her previous clients, she eventually found a surgeon who would attempt to remove the cataract. Sympathetic to Ann's financial situation, the doctor donated his services and covered the operating room costs.

The surgery to restore her sight was extremely high risk. It could destroy whatever sight she still had in her left eye if done wrong. Before her surgery, Ann reportedly told her doctor, "If I can't design dresses, I'd rather fly off the Empire State Building, so please do not disappoint me."

The August 1964 operation was a success, restoring sight to Ann's left eye. After recuperating for two months, Ann was ready to get back to work. She was grateful that her sister Sallie could run her shop while recovering. When a 66-year-old Ann returned to her shop, she hired an assistant to help reestablish her clientele. According to *The Saturday Evening Post*, Ann and her assistant wrote 500 handwritten postcards to reconnect with previous customers. The strategy worked, and Ann was sewing for several previous customers. She continued to create wholesale designs and maintained her close and personalized working style with her couture clients.

# Chapter Twenty-Five

# THE WEDDING DESIGNER

***"The funny thing about your gift is, it never leaves you. It doesn't matter if you use it every day or haven't used it in years. It always remembers you." – Ann Lowe***

In 1964, Ann Copeland, a frequent client of Ann's, commissioned her to design her wedding dress. When Copeland arrived at Ann's dress shop, she was surprised at what she saw. In an interview with the New York Gazette, Copeland recalled what it was like watching Ann work after her eye surgery: "Her assistants hovered around her to be certain that she got it all right. Ms. Lowe was very frail but still so gentle and talented. No one made dresses as beautifully," Copeland said.

The amount of sewing that Ann could complete on her own on this gown is unclear. Still, it's not surprising to hear that Ann's advancing age and health problems brought Copeland to worry at times that she would "never see the final product." When she asked Ann if she could also make the bridesmaid's dresses, Copeland

noticed that one of Ann's assistants "gave me a nod, clearly indicating not to let her do them…she was simply not up to it; by then."

Ann was not feeling well enough to make ten more dresses for the wedding. Fortunately, the maid of honor, the bridesmaids, and the two flower girls' dresses were designed by another design house to coordinate with the dress that Ann was making. According to the *New York Times*, "all the attendants were gowned in long ivory linen dresses made with empire waistlines," said Copeland.

"The amount of revenue Ann missed by having to pass on designing ten additional dresses was substantial and a sign that even with this fresh start, things were beginning to fall out of place. It would be difficult not to compare this experience to the height of Ann's career when she could outfit an entire wedding party or Gasparilla court without a problem. Fortunately, Ann Copeland's gown was finished on time and without incident, and the results were perfect, said historian Margaret Powell. "The dress was fabulous!" Copeland recalled.

Ann designed her clients' wedding dresses, but her shop also gave her clients a complete wedding experience. Ann's dress shop provided full service, door-to-door staff assistance on the day of the bride's wedding. During this time, the designer of a high-profile wedding like Ann Copeland's usually provided one-one service.

Ann and her staff added a personal touch by going to Copeland's home to help her dress. "It was a rainy day, and the team assisted her while she entered the car by holding umbrellas for her.

This was an expected part of a couture wedding gown experience and a service that Ann provided herself in Tampa when she "was present to straighten out the veils as the brides began their walk down the church aisle" during weddings throughout the 1920s. This stands as a testament to Ann's character to see that she could still maintain her competitor's customer service standards while facing many personal challenges. "The simplicity of Copeland's wedding gown without all the embroidery flowers, tulle, and big bouffant skirt, implies that Lowe was transitioning away from the intricate ball gowns that were going out of style during the late 1960s," said Margret Powell.

*The Copeland wedding gown is a part of the permanent collection of the Delaware Historical Society in Wilmington, Delaware. It will be a valuable modern example of Ann's work to study alongside the more traditional ball gowns in the Metropolitan Museum of Art collection that feature large skirts and portrait neckline bodices.*

It brought Ann great joy designing dresses for old clients. The love she received from them gave her the confidence to keep doing what she loved doing. Ann loved to reminiscence about the old days of designing for prominent socialites in New York. One socialite she

thought about often was Mrs. Kennedy. In an interview with the *Saturday Evening Post* in 1964, Ann spoke about how "sweet" Jackie was to her. "My great-grandmother told close friends how nice Mrs. Kennedy was to her when designing her wedding dress. Ann also told close friends how disappointed she was that she never received the proper recognition for designing Mrs. Kennedy's wedding gown. I believe she carried that disappointment with her for the rest of her life," says great-granddaughter Linda.

# Chapter Twenty-Six

# GOING TO HOLLYWOOD

***"I love my clothes, and I'm particular about who wears them. I am not interested in sewing for cafe society or social climbers. I do not cater to Mary and Sue. I sew for the families of the Social Register." – Ann Lowe***

In late 1964, Ann received some news that would make her face and name known to millions. Ann's old friend, Lena Horne, asked her to make a gown for her and bring it to Los Angeles, where Horne was scheduled to perform. Ann delivered the dress to Horne while working on a soundstage in Hollywood.

While visiting Ms. Horne, Ann ran into a producer for the then-popular television show, the Mike Douglas show. Ann and the producer struck up a conversation. Ann told the producer that she was the one who designed Jackie Kennedy's wedding dress. Intrigued by her story, the producer convinced Mike Douglas to have Ann on his show. Ann appeared on the Mike Douglas Show on December 22, 1964.

When Ann returned to New York from Los Angles, she sat down with a reporter from the *Saturday Evening Post* who asked her how she came up with her fabulous designs. Ann replied, "I believe I get my inspiration from God. I cannot explain it any other way." She went on to say what she likes for her customers to feel when wearing one of her gowns, "I like for my dresses to be admired. I like to hear about the oohs and ahs as they come into the ballroom. Like when someone tells me, 'the Ann Lowe dresses were doing all the dancing at the cotillion last night.' That's what I like to hear."

With the ball gown era slowly ending and her financial situation looking bleak, Ann was delighted to receive a phone call that would help her out finically. In April of 1965, Baroness Walter Langer von Langendorff of the Evyan Perfume Collection commissioned Ann to design and dress six "First Lady" dolls that represented the wives of six presidents of the United States.

While the original full-size gowns were already on display in the Smithsonian Institution's First Ladies gown collection, Ann's miniature dresses were made to be displayed in high-end department stores while promoting the fragrances, *Great Lady* and *White Shoulders*. The campaign was a huge success, which gave a financially struggling Ann a much-needed financial boost she needed to invest in the last big venture of her life.

# Chapter Twenty-Seven

# YOU'RE NEVER TOO OLD

***"Even at my age, I still have dreams I want to fulfill." – Ann Lowe***

While most people enjoy retirement in their late sixties, Ann was busy fulfilling a lifelong dream. In 1966, at 68, with the help of designer Florence Cowell, Ann opened her final dress shop, *"Ann Lowe's Originals,"* on Fifth Avenue. Ann's lifelong dream was to open a dress shop on the prestigious Fifth Avenue, and she finally did it. Ann made history as the first black woman to open a dress shop on Fifth Avenue. When Ann joined forces with designer Cowell, she made sure that Cowell knew she was the one in charge. "I'm going to do this myself," Ann told Cowell. "No one is going to take from me what is not theirs. This time, I will get paid what I'm worth."

In 1966, *Ebony* sat down with the busy fashion designer in her new atelier to discover how she stayed on top of the fashion industry. Ann said, "You must always be creating in the world of fashion, or else people will forget about you very quickly. That's why I don't

believe in taking time off. I work all the time. That's why I was able to turn out an average of 1,000 gowns a year at one time. With a staff of 35 and grossed $300,000 annually, you always have to be working." When asked how she felt about the media calling her the 'first black fashion designer,' Ann responded, "I like it very much."

Ann's new shop was lavishly decorated with white and gold. The exquisitely designed walls were immersed with bold and colorful flowers, which she designed herself. She had a photo wall dedicated to her famous clientele, whom she loved dearly. Many of her sketches of the dresses she created over the years were also located around her shop.

Ann continued to design her "fairy-tale princess" style gowns in her new shop, even though styles for debutantes were changing. In 1967, *Vanity Fair* featured a chic dress designed by Ann. The coverage refreshed her business with fashions more relevant to young women in the Civil Rights Movement and the Vietnam War era. "The girls want more fitting-in at the waist," Ann told the *New York Times* in 1967 when reporter Virginia Lee Warren visited her shop to ask about her newest looks. "Last year, they wanted a shallow scoop or even a tank-top neckline. Now, if it isn't a low back, it's the portrait, deep off-the-shoulder one," Ann said. When a customer asked Ann why the fabric in the back of her dresses was usually almost nonexistent, the designer, who always wore a black fedora while she worked, said, "To save my beautiful dresses; I want

to keep the hands of the boys from getting them so dirty when they dance."

In 1967, *Ann Lowe's Original* gowns were priced between $200 and $995, with the average price for a debutante gown being between $395 and $495." This is compared to her prices in 1957, when Ann was not always comfortable with her pricing structure; she charged "up to $500" for her gowns."Prices went up in 1968 when her gowns could be purchased on a walk-in basis, and her custom gowns ranged from $695-$795. Ann was able to build upon her success with a revised pricing structure, a strong and highly skilled staff, and a new modern outlook on her dress designs. She continued to bring Ann Lowe's gowns into a new period of growth and success," said historian Margaret Powell.

Ann was thrilled when one of her debutante gowns was featured along with her name in a *Town and Country* magazine. The recognition gave Ann a sense of accomplishment. Seeing her designed and being recognized for her designs brought Ann great joy. Ann created no more high-profile gowns during the late sixties, but she was still selling several debutante gowns through high-end department stores around the country and the business from her Fifth Ave shop.

While 1967 brought Ann great success, it also brought her great sorrow when her beloved sister, Sallie, died in September 1967. Ann

was devastated. She had lost her big sister, protector, and biggest fan. Ann and Sallie were very close sisters. Sallie was Ann's saving grace after Arthur died. The two lived together until Sallie's death. Sallie's death was announced in the *New York Times*.

By 1968, Ann's work pace had slowed down dramatically. She was no longer the eighteen-year-old designer who could design and complete a fancy dress in one day, the way she could during the height of her career in Tampa. By this time, Ann was constantly surrounded by assistants who helped her with the everyday task of designing and sewing gowns. Ann was the face of the brand.

# Chapter Twenty-Eight

# BOWING OUT GRACEFULLY

***"It's always good to know when it's time to leave the party."***

***– Ann Lowe***

In 1971, Ann's eyesight and health were drastically fading. It was clear to everyone around her that her career was slowly ending. Ann finally retired and closed the doors to her shop on Madison Ave in 1972.

Unable to live independently because of her failing eyesight, Ann moved in with her adopted daughter, Ruth Williams Alexander, on Long Island. "I thank God that my grandmother Ruth could take in my great-grandmother. At the time, my mother, Audrey, wasn't doing well enough to take in my great-grandmother, so I'm glad grandmother Ruth was there for her. I remember visiting my great-grandmother. She would sit and talk for hours about the elaborate debutante and wedding gowns she had designed over the years. But

the main thing she would talk about was her son, Arthur," said great-granddaughter Linda.

At the end of her career, Ann received numerous local honors in New York City during the 1970s. In 1976, she was honored with a luncheon and fashion show held in her honor by an African American Fraternity, Alpha Phi Alpha. This final show dedicated exclusively to Ann Lowe's work showcased many dresses Ann created in the 1940s and 1950s. The citation read at the event highlighted her accomplishments:

*"An American and international designer whose life has been filled with sagas of patience, sadness, and happiness, she has dressed First Ladies of the nation. There is no resentment of the illnesses, tragedies, and financial problems that beset her. She opened her first salon with a borrowed $20,000, and soon her name became synonymous with elegance and beauty. She has provided clothing for the grand entrances of some of the most celebrated ladies of our land."*

Ann could not attend the event, but several family members were in attendance and her granddaughter, an aspiring fashion designer named Audrey Hassell, accepted the plaque on Ann's behalf. It seems very fitting that Ann's final interview was given to the *Tampa Tribune* to benefit the Tampa residents, who had been such an essential part of her early career. Betty Phipps, the *Tribune* reporter, met Ann to discuss the Alpha Phi Alpha luncheon.

Ann was completely blind at this point, and when she was presented with the plaque from the banquet to honor her life achievements, Phipps noted that "Ann ran her fingers over the plaque, the heavy wood frame, the brass plate set on velvet, her fingers outlined the engraving. Ann said softly, "This is such a wonderful blessing. There are still a thousand ideas I have for dresses in my mind. Dresses which I see in great detail. Some days I can see them clearly, and some days I can't see them at all."

While taking care of Ann, Ruth wrote in her journal how a few of Ann's loyal clients sent money to help with her living expenses during Ann's final years. Ruth, a loving daughter, made sure Ann was well taken care of. After an extended illness, Ann Lowe died quietly in her sleep on February 25, 1981. She was 82 years old.

Like her life, Ann's funeral was described as a quiet and dignified Harlem funeral, held at the prestigious St. Mark's United Methodist Church in Manhattan, where Ann was a longtime member. Reports suggest that her services were paid for by her friend and benefactor, Baroness Walter von Langendorff of the Evyan Perfume Company. "Her funeral was fitting for a woman of her style and grace," said great-granddaughter Linda. Ann is buried at Ferncliff Cemetery in Hartsdale, New York. Also buried at Ferncliff are Malcolm X and James Baldwin.

Ann Lowe's name is still virtually unknown, with over a thousand gowns made in her life for some of the wealthiest women in American history. Hopefully, as more of her designs are rediscovered, more people will know about the fabulous yet underrated career of Ann Lowe.

# Chapter Twenty-Nine

# A LEGACY LIVES ON

***"Of all the pleasures I have ever known, sewing has been the greatest." – Ann Lowe***

The legacy of Ann Lowe was once hidden in plain sight, not entirely accepted nor fully acknowledged, but today, her story is no longer fashion's best-kept secret. Some of her designs are preserved at renowned museums with a newfound interest in Ann. Her collections can be seen at the Metropolitan Museum of Art, the Museum of the City of New York, and the Smithsonian National Museum of African American History and Culture, where Smithsonian curator Elaine Nichols reflects on Ann's creative designs, "She was exceptional, and her work moves you."

Ann's designs can also be seen at The Museum at the Fashion Institute of Technology (MFIT) in Manhattan."Her work was overwhelmingly pretty," says Elizabeth Way of the Fashion Institute of Technology. "It wasn't radical or meant to be. Even in the sixties,

she was still inspired by the nineteenth century and a nostalgic ideal of femininity. Yet, I also think it's important to appreciate what breathtaking courage she had."

Ann's fabulous wedding dress for Mrs. Kennedy is now preserved at the John F. Kennedy Presidential Library. The fragile condition of Jackie Kennedy's wedding dress has prevented it from being displayed in recent years. A full-sized replica designed by artist Isabella de Borchgrave was created for the library in 2004. The replica includes all of the decorative elements of the original gown as closely as possible. The replica version is more suitable for long-term public display, allowing generations of visitors to view the dramatic effect of Ann's design long after the original silk gown became too fragile to be displayed.

In 2005, Ann's twenty-eight miniature gowns for Baroness Walter Langer von Langendorff of the Evyan Perfume Collection were donated to the National First Ladies Library in Canton, Ohio. Because of the fragility of the gowns, they require special care and are not always on open display, but when they are, they are displayed in the order of the presidential administrations. These 41-inch replicas are extremely popular with guests at the First Ladies' Library, and the staff strives to always have at least three of them on exhibit at a time while the remaining dresses 'rest' to preserve the delicate fabric.

Today, we applaud Ann Lowe for being a true trailblazer, a daring entrepreneur, a dedicated artist, and a fashion force to be reckoned with.

# Chapter Thirty

# REMEMBERING ANN LOWE

***"I did not become a dressmaker to be rich or famous. I did it to be a positive representative for my people. It was always my desire to prove that a Negro woman could become a major dress designer; I believe I have done that exceptionally well." – Ann Lowe***

Ann Lowe's name still may not be as famous as other fashion designers, yet her contributions to the fashion world should be recognized and celebrated. As a black American

woman trying to make a name for herself in the predominantly white fashion industry when America was dealing with racial segregation, Ann fought hard against racism to become America's first black female haute couture designer. Because of her skin color, Ann had to endure a lot of discrimination, with several white-owned fashion

houses refusing to fairly compensate her for her work or giving her credit for her designs.

Life wasn't always easy for the little woman with big dreams from Montgomery, Alabama, but she used her sewing gift to rise above poverty and racial injustice. With success came personal tragedy, financial disasters, and business setbacks, but Ann weathered each storm in her life with resilience. She worked tirelessly so that her designs would be accepted, appreciated, and valued; she wanted these same things for herself in many ways.

Ann created her own opportunities, which led her to become the first black female haute couture designer to have a dress shop on the prestigious Madison Ave. She opened doors, so others who looked like her didn't have to use back doors anymore. The tiny country girl who made it from the dirt roads of Montgomery, Alabama, to the bright streets of New York dared to push beyond the limitations and expectations placed on her by a racially divided society.

Ann Lowe's life story lies beneath layers of fabric woven together through adversity, triumphs, and personal tragedy. But her story is just one thread of countless unsung African Americans whose contributions to America have either faded or never made it into American History books. To ignore parts of our history is to ignore parts of ourselves. So, to fully embrace who we are, we must first learn where we have been, where we are now, and what we must do

to get where we are going. We honor Ann Lowe for being a courageous trailblazer, a daring entrepreneur, a dedicated artist, and a fashion force to be reckoned with. I hope her name will rise once again and claim its proper place where it rightfully belongs in American History.

# ACKNOWLEDGMENTS

Linda A. Dixon – Ann Lowe's Great-Granddaughter

Lewis Cole (Cousin)

Margaret E. Powell – Writer/Textile Historian

Ann Lowe - Hidden Fashion History -2016

The Life and Work of Ann Lowe: Rediscovering "Society's Best Kept Secret"

By Margaret Eugenia Powell

hiddenfashionhistory.com

Lois K. Alexander Lane -Black Fashion Museum

"Ann Lowe's Early Career." Elizabeth Way, Fashion Historian - The Fashion Institute of Technology

"Threads of Time: The Fabric of History" –Rosemary E. Reed Miller/Historian T & S Press, 2002.

Elaine Nichols - N.M.A.A.H.C.

Black Fashion Museum. **1979-2007**, Smithsonian National Museum of African American History and Culture, Washington, D.C.

The Saturday Evening Post-1964

Marissa Henderson

Ann Lowe: America's Overlooked Fashion Icon Finally Found

Congdon, Thomas "Ann Lowe: Society's Best Kept Secret." Saturday Evening Post, 12 Dec. 1964 Lowe, Ann. Letter to Jacqueline Kennedy, 5 Apr. 1961.

Ann Lowe Hidden Fashion History. Major, Gerri. "Dean of Fashion Designers." Ebony Magazine, Dec. 1966

McAndrew, Malia. "A Twentieth-Century Triangle Trade: Selling Black Beauty at Home and Abroad, 1945–1965." Enterprise & Society, vol. 11, no. 4, 2010.

"The Life and Work of Ann Lowe: Rediscovering Society's Best Kept Secret." Dissertation, The Smithsonian Associates and The Corcoran College of Art and Design, 2012

Ann Lowe's Barrier-Breaking Mid-Century Couture by Judith Thurman *(The New Yorker)*

Ann Cole Lowe | Profiles in Sewing History the African American seamstress designed Jacqueline Kennedy's wedding dress By Dana Finkle (THREADS)

Brockell, Gillian. "Jackie Kennedy's fairy-tale wedding was a nightmare for her African American dress designer." *The Washington Post*,

WP Company, Aug. 28, 2019

Phipps, Betty. "Ann Cone Lowe: A Tampa Legacy Is Honored in New York." The Tampa Tribune, 7 Aug. 1976, pp. 12-13.

Kwateng-Clark, Danielle. "How a Little-Known Black Pioneer Changed Fashion Forever." *Racked*, Sept. 30, 2016

Ann Smith. "Ann Lowe Couturier to the Rich and Famous,"

*Alabama Heritage* 53 (1999)

Laneri, Raquel. "Why Jackie Kennedy's wedding dress designer was fashion's 'best-kept secret.'" *New York Post*, Oct. 16, 2016.

Major, Gerri. "Ebony.", Johnson Publishing Company, Dec. 1966.

*Google Books*

Nancy Davis. "Sewing for joy: Ann Lowe." *National Museum of American History*, March 12, 2018.

Powell, Margaret. "The Life and Work of Ann Lowe: Rediscovering 'Society's Best-Kept Secret'," Master's thesis for The Smithsonian Associates and the Corcoran College of Art & Design, 2012.

"Pretty in Pink." *National Museum of African American History and Culture*, July 5, 2019

"The Remarkable Story of Ann Lowe: From Alabama to Madison Avenue." National Archives and Records Administration, National Archives and Records Administration, 2013.

Wilson, Julee. "Ann Lowe: Black Fashion Designer Who Created Jacqueline Kennedy's Wedding Dress," *HuffPost*, Dec. 6, 2017

**Photos Courtesy of:**

Naila Ruechel for The New Yorker

EBONY Magazine

JET Magazine

LIFE Magazine

Getty Images

Smithsonian National Museum of African American History Collection of the and Culture

The Henry Plant Museum, Tampa Florida

Ann Lowe Gowns Courtesy © The Museum at FIT

Geri Major, "Dean of American Designers," *Ebony*, December 1966

State of Alabama Department of Education, Literacy, and Illiteracy in Alabama, 1914

J. Paul Getty Trust

Bachrach / Getty

Bettmann / Getty

Lisa Larsen / Getty

Johnson Publishing Company Archive.

Courtesy Ford Foundation

John D. and Catherine T. MacArthur Foundation

Andrew W. Mellon Foundation and Smithsonian Institution

Noemi Bonazzi

Discover the beautiful and original designs of Ann Lowe, one of the most innovative fashion designers in American History, in a new exciting, colorful photobook,

***ANN LOWE'S ORIGINAL DESIGNS***

available at amazon.com

# ABOUT THE AUTHOR

Pier Angela Belton is an author, producer, and screenwriter. A college graduate, her passion for Black History, African American films, and African American literature have influenced her to write a collection of books focusing on the history of African American women in the movie, education, business,

and fashion industry. She was a freelance writer for Response magazine in New York. She produced an online monthly inspirational lifestyle magazine, Inspire Entertainment. She worked on many films sets for Warner Brothers Studios, where she had the opportunity to work with great directors like Barry Levinson and Ryan Coogler. She has written several screenplays and documentaries. She enjoys visiting museums, traveling, and reading. Ms. Belton lives in Northern California.

*Author's Contact Information:*

**BELTON MEDIA ONE**


Pier Angela Belton

mspabelton@gmail.com

www.beltonmedia.co


*Books * Screenplays * Documentaries*

# Books from the

# <u>***Colored Couture Collection***</u>

**The Evolution of Black Female Fashion Designers**

**From Slave to Seamstress**
***Ona Judges, Elizabeth Keckley, Fannie Criss, and Rosa Parks***
***(Coming Summer 2022)***

**The Evolution of Black Female Fashion Designers**

**The Life Story of Ann Lowe (available now)**
**The Original Designs of Ann Lowe (Photo Book) (available now)**

**The Evolution of Black Female Fashion Designers**

<u>**Couture, Costumes, and Culture**</u>
***Fashion Designer Zelda Wynn***
***(Coming Summer 2022)***

<u>**The Evolution of Black Female Fashion Designers**</u>

**Hats Off to You**
***Mildred Blount***
***(Coming Summer 2022)***

## Black Beauty Books

***(Coming Summer 2022)***

The Glamour of Dorothy Dandridge

The Glamour of Lena Horne

The Soulful Sex Symbol – Joyce Bryant

## Black Culture Books

Black, Bold, and Beautiful: Blaxploitation Beauties

***(Coming Fall 2022)***

Black Hollywood
From House Maid to Having It Made
***(Coming Fall 2022)***

Made in the USA
Monee, IL
11 September 2023

f269090d-2289-4c09-a960-49260d073132R01